MW00387230

High-Performance SAS® Coding

Third Edition

Brett D. Johnson
[585]
880-4439

To my family, I would be nothing without them.

Thank you to Alex Whitehouse for his fantastic help with the editing, to Andrew Cathie for his thoughtful and much appreciated comments, to Franco Pierantoni for his encouragements, to Roseline Fernandes for being such a wonderful and supporting friend, to the good people of Sysware (www.syswaregroup.com) in New Zealand and of Decision Networks (www.decision-network.eu) in France for their support along the years, and to SAS Institute for creating a fabulous piece of software!

And mostly thank you to you, dear reader, for trusting me with your time by reading this book.

Legal Notes

Copyright © 2019 by Christian Graffeuille

Feel free to reuse or quote small excerpts of this book, provided you fully name the source (title, author, ISBN) each time.

I have occasionally quoted a few sentences from the SAS documentation when I thought they were concise, clear and pertinent. I have endeavoured to name the reference each time. Likewise, I have sometimes been inspired by existing material. Again, I have endeavoured to give a comprehensive bibliography. Please contact me if I forgot something.

SAS® and all other SAS Institute Inc. product or service names are registered trademarks or trademarks of SAS Institute Inc. in the USA and other countries.

® indicates USA registration. Other brand and product names are registered trademarks or trademarks of their respective companies.

Contents

Illustrations

Tables

Conventions

SAS code is shown in frames, in colour for the polychrome edition.

```
data T5E6(sortedby=I);
  do I=1 to 5e6;
    output;
  end;
run;
```

Log messages are shown in frames using the SAS Monospace font:

```
NOTE: DATA statement used (Total process time):
      real time            3.89 seconds
```

This icon shows a remark or a noteworthy feature about the topic reviewed:

☞ As a reminder…

This icon highlights a feature from my wish list that is sorely missing in the SAS software; I use the opportunity of this book to publicise my plea to the SAS developers.

🖐 Please SAS Institute: …

The red flag highlights a potential pitfall:

⚑ **Danger: …**

Chapter 1

About This Book

Background

I like technology. I became a mechanical engineer because I've always liked to make things work as best as they can. I appreciate sleek and efficient systems, whatever they may be; be it as humble as the US phone plug (how the European ones look awkward and clunky in comparison) or as advanced as Yamaha's fracture-split method for manufacturing titanium connecting rods. Smart, simple, elegant things! Because I like high-performance engines (of any kind), I have a KTM SX300 motocross bike which I utilise well under its potential, but whose raw power gives me unending thrills.

So that's what drives the author: I have a bit of OCD with technological performance and efficiency. Not that my dear wife would recognize this border-line obsession with everything falling into place in my everyday life....

As a SAS user, this means that I have always sought to write resource-efficient code, and that I have gained a bit of knowledge around this topic. So when SAS Publications made a call for authors, I thought I'd give it a go and write a book about SAS programming, but with a twist: its emphasis would be on performance. I have seen many SAS programs in my career, and the majority were badly written and could often run an order of magnitude faster or more by being better organised and by using SAS features that few SAS developers use. Additionally, slow code is often convoluted and difficult to maintain as it goes on and on with a multitude of steps calling each other's results without a visible overall design. I can't address the design issue here, but I can show efficient coding and hope to encourage leaner, cleaner, more efficient code to make the world a more efficient place.

Purpose

This book is all about performance, or at least it should be. Its purpose is to enhance the speed of SAS programmers' code. There are always many ways to realise one task in SAS, and some are better than others. Most SAS training (rightly) focuses on teaching coding, and code performance is seldom the emphasis: There are enough things to learn without studying the intricacies of what's happening behind the scene, or which solutions work better for which situation. This book is here to shed light on how things work, what SAS options and statements do, when to use them for best performance.

Is This Book for You?

This book is intended for SAS programmers. These are a slow-growing breed these days, as most SAS users have to use Enterprise Guide. The other side of the coin of course is that those users who make the effort to learn the SAS language are fewer and therefore more sought after. If SAS programmers also know how to speed up the processes that sometime seem to take forever to complete, or how to write efficient code that takes advantage of both the hardware available and the many SAS features and options, their path to a great career is bordered with tap-dancing wide-eyed pink fluffy unicorns and covered in lotus petals. Yes it will!

Prerequisites

This book will not teach you how to program using SAS. If you know how to program however, you will gain a wealth of knowledge. You'll learn what your code does behind the scenes, what options can be used to alter its behaviour, in short how to improve your code's performance.

Organisation

This is the first chapter; it contains some information about the book itself.

The second chapter gives an overview about computer hardware and how it is used by the software. Making a program efficient simply means making a program use fewer hardware resources, so knowledge about hardware is essential. Yet few programmers have this background knowledge. If you know your cache and your queue length, or if you just don't have the time, the second chapter is optional.

The third chapter contains reminders about how to use SAS (but many tips apply to other data processing tools). This will make for a light reading for the more seasoned programmers, but omitting this basic knowledge in a book all about performance would have left a gap. Experienced programmers will recognise common mistakes, while newer ones will learn important tips.

The fourth chapter is about sorting and PROC SORT. It endeavours to be the complete, once-and-for-all, source of information for programmers. It explains how PROC SORT works and how to tweak it for best performance. This is ambitious. I hope I have succeeded to a certain degree.

The fifth chapter presents the main SAS options that can affect the speed of a program. It is possible that changing an option, with no other modification, halves the processing time as shown in some examples.

The sixth chapter presents some aspects of the SPDE engine.

The seventh chapter is new to third edition of this book and lets us delve into table joins.

The last chapter presents How SAS can use Regular Expressions, the power house of string manipulation.

I want to cover more topics such as: sequential jobs vs parallel jobs (including PROC DS2 and MP CONNECT), pipes and named pipes, but this will have to wait a bit longer....

Output and Graphs Used in This Book

All the graphs in this book are produced using SAS.

About the Examples

I have chosen to show SAS code as part of the text rather than in appendixes. It means that reading the book demands a bit more attention than just browsing a text-only explanation, but it enables readers to see exactly how the benchmarks are conducted.

The examples, tests and benchmarks in this book were ran on a variety of machines small to large, using versions of SAS ranging from 9.1 to 9.4 and operating systems including Windows 32, Windows 64, AIX, HP-UX. They should give similar results in your environment but may not always do so. I found that the biggest factor influencing repeatability across platforms was the performance of the I/O subsystems. In particular, changing from spinning disks to solid state disks can render some optimization tips less effective or even counter-productive. This is because SSDs have fast random-access times, and the tips attempting to reduce slow I/O operations are fighting an absent foe.

In any case, each program, each data set, each machine is different. The many benchmarks provided here are not only to demonstrate the effects of the SAS settings reviewed, but mostly to give you a running start in your quest for performance.

Get in Touch

You can reach me at %substr(&book_title,1,9)@graffeuille.org if you want to discuss the book's contents. If you notice any error, want to make constructive comments, discuss a point, please write there. I'll do my best to reply in a timely fashion.

Chapter 2

Hardware: what is performance?

Chapter 2

Hardware: what is performance?

Introduction

If you understand your hardware you can probably just skip this chapter. You may want to browse through to ensure you are not missing anything, as I delve into relevant details here and there, and you may pick up new bits of knowledge. If you are just not interested at all about hardware, you can skip this chapter altogether, though a few explanations later in the book might be harder to follow.

It's all nice and good to talk about performance, but what does it mean concretely? How does good performance translate in terms of actual, physical events? What is happening inside a computer that makes a process slow or fast? How does a process run? To understand performance, we must understand to some extend what's under the hood. Let's have a look.

In order to run and process data, software needs the following resources:

- A place to store data permanently,
- A place to store data that is currently processed,
- A processor to do something with or to that data.

Storage

Ideally, there would only be one type of data storage: a cheap media that is as fast as the processor needs and holds the data when it is powered off. Unfortunately, such media does not exist. Therefore, and because of technological constraints, storage is divided into cheaper and slower permanent storage, and faster and costlier volatile (i.e. non-permanent) storage.

Permanent storage

Data access operations done on permanently stored data are the slowest, and are very important for SAS processes. These operations are called IO (for Input-Output) operations.

Permanent storage media will store data even when it is not electrically powered. As far as SAS usage is concerned, permanent on-line storage is typically made on Hard Disk Drives or HDDs. HDDs have the benefit of being cheap, and offer a large storage capacity for a reasonable price. Hard disks store data as magnetic information on spinning platters.

For higher-speed permanent storage, hard disks are being replaced by Solid State Drives or SSDs. Solid state drives use flash memory, which is non-volatile and is made of silicon chips. Solid state drives are much faster than hard disk drives –and more expensive– but nowhere near as fast as volatile memory.

Solid-state technology is now cheap enough that many SAS customers use it for their WORK libraries, and a growing number of customers also use it for their permanent SAS libraries.

Volatile storage (memory)

Volatile means ephemeral or transitory or non-permanent. Volatile storage is called that because it needs to be powered in order to work. Cut the power and all the data is gone. Volatile storage in computers is also called Random Access Memory or RAM, or just "memory" for short. RAM is made of silicon chips, and for the same storage space is much more expensive than permanent storage. RAM is several orders of magnitude faster than hard disks and the price ratio is similar.

Because of this difference in speed, a computer's memory can spend a lot of time waiting for data coming from the drives.

Processor

Processors (their proper name is Central Processing Units or CPUs) execute programs. All programs, regardless how they were created, are translated into a set of processor instructions. When programs ask for data, processors read data from the computer's RAM. If the data isn't there, the data is fetched from the permanent storage media, which creates IO operations.

Processors typically run at a higher frequency than the memory does, and can spend a lot of time waiting for data coming from the RAM.

Caching

Caching is an essential performance feature of computer systems. Fast CPUs talk to slower RAM. The RAM talks to the slower hard disks' electronics. And finally the data is retrieved from the slowest medium: the spinning platters.

In order to alleviate the faster components' waiting for the slower ones, faster components incorporate what is called memory caches. These caches are small storage spaces used to store data in the hope that the next time the fast component needs data, this data will already be in the cache and will not have to be fetched from the slower component down the chain.

So the CPU caches memory data and the memory caches hard disk data. More caches can be added at each intermediate step such as in the hard disk controller and in the hard disk's electronics. Caching makes much difference in the performance of the various components, and is most often hardware-based. This means there isn't much you can do to tweak how caching works. Only the memory cache, which is normally managed by the Operating System and sits between the storage subsystem and the processor, can be changed. We will discuss how caching disk data, or not, can be used to SAS's advantage.

Permanent Storage

Permanent storage is probably the most important component of any machine running SAS. SAS usually has to process a large quantity of data, and all too often it is the storage subsystem that slows things down. SAS jobs can typically run faster if the data can be stored or retrieved faster. On SAS machines, fast storage is a must.

Storage technology is varied and can take many forms. Before we delve into the specifics of each technology, we should understand a few performance parameters that are common to any storage medium.

Hard Disk Storage

The vast majority of online SAS data is stored on hard disks. A storage medium's performance can be measured for two types of actions: read and write, and for 2 types of operations: random access and sequential access. This is true of Hard Disk Drives (HDDs) as well as other storage means like solid state drives or even tape drives. We'll focus on hard disk drives first, since they are so prevalent, but the principle is true for all storage mechanisms. We'll look at Solid State Drives in a further section.

Read vs. Write speeds.

Reading data is typically faster than writing data since writing involves modifying data, whereas reading simply involves retrieving data with no alteration of the storage system. Some data storage systems are especially penalising when writing as we'll see below.

Random Access vs. Sequential Access

Two main types of performance measures are used to assess the speed of a data storage system: the time it takes to retrieve a small and random piece of data, and the transfer speed to read or write as much data as possible in a continuous manner.

Access Time

The first measure, that measures how long it takes to access a small random piece of data, is called access time.

For hard drives -and for all rotating storage medium for that matter- access time is essentially a combination of two durations called seek time and rotational latency, and is measured in milliseconds. Typical access times vary from 5 to 30 ms depending on the hard disk.

Seek time is the time it takes for the read-write head to go across the spinning medium to the circular track containing the data. The smaller the spinning platter containing data, the less the head has to move and the faster seek time will be. One common method for speeding up seek time on an existing hard disk is to reduce its capacity. By not making the whole disk available for data storage, only part of the platter is used, and the distance the head has to travel to go from data to data is reduced. This method is called short-stroking.

Rotational latency (or latency) is the time it takes for the medium to spin and bring the right data under the read-write head. On average, latency is the time it takes to effect one-half of a rotation. The only way to speed this up is to spin the platters faster. The faster, enterprise-grade, hard disks spin at 15,000 revolutions per minute (RPM) and that's the hard disks your SAS machines should be using.

Data transfer rate

The second measure, which uses the time it takes to sequentially read or write a large piece of data, is called throughput speed. It is also called data transfer rate. Once the head is positioned over the data, the disk can start streaming data in a continuous manner as long as the data is stored sequentially from that position. The throughput speed is measured in megabytes per second. Typical hard disk throughput speeds vary from 100 to 200 MB/s.

Two factors influence the throughput speed: rotational speed and areal density, i.e. how fast the disk platter flies by the read-write head (that's the rotational speed, again) and how much data a unit of area (for example a square millimetre or a square inch) holds.

☞ Note that the head never touches the platter. If it were to touch it, it would damage it and the hard disk would be irreversibly damaged. To prevent the head from crashing into the platter, a small wedge of air is created by the speed of the spinning platter, and is pushed between the platter surface and the head. This air cushion lifts the head a few nanometres (less than a thousandth of a hair's diameter) above the platter while the platter surface travels at around 100 mph right under the head. No room for error (or dust, or wobbly platters, or hard knocks) there!

Now that we understand how to measure the performance of a storage system, we can look at various ways to improve it.

Solid State Storage

One way to speed up the storage system is to use solid-state storage. Contrarily to hard disk drives, Solid State Drives (SSDs) have no moving parts, they are purely electronic. There is no waiting for platters to spin or arms to move before accessing data. For this reason, their access times are much faster than hard disk access times: About 100 to 1,000 times faster! That's a colossal improvement. As the technology matures, the transfer rates are also steadily increasing and SSDs are now faster than HDDs in this respect as well.

With these incredible speed gains, why would anyone still use hard disks? Well, there are few reasons. SSDs are not without downsides.

Firstly, they are costlier than HDDs for the same storage capacity.

Secondly they wear out. The number of times they can write data in any given cell is limited. After this limit has been reached, the reliability of data retention deteriorates. Hard disks don't have this problem. So if the SSD does a lot of writes, as for example the SASWORK library entails, this will have to be considered.

Thirdly, they have limitations when rewriting data, because they cannot simply replace a cell's data with updated data. The cell must be erased first. All good then, you say, erase and overwrite. Well, SSDs don't know how to erase single cells yet; they erase blocks of cells instead. On a hard disk, a piece of data that has changed is simply overwritten and that's it. On a SSD, what usually happens is that the old cell is marked as old and the new data is written elsewhere. When the SSD needs more free space, it looks for blocks with many cells marked old, it moves the good data elsewhere, erases the block of cells and marks them as available again. This limitation causes a few issues:

- It triggers more write operations thereby increasing wear
- The block-erase operation takes time and can delay processes if not done in the background.
- The location of the data on the disk is not managed by the Operating System any more since the SSD doesn't overwrite data in place, but instead uses available cells wherever they are. This has two repercussions. For one, it means that free-space management must be handled differently than with conventional hard disk storage (using processes called Garbage Collection, and the TRIM command). It also means that because data is scattered all over the drive, data recovery is often impossible in case of drive failure. Note that even if single cells could be erased, the problem would still exist and SSDs would still not replace and overwrite data in place. The reason is the wear-out issue. You wouldn't want the same sector overwritten over and over while other sectors remain unused, as is the case with hard-disks, since this sector would quickly wear out and become unusable. So a wear-levelling policy is in place to ensure all sectors are used equally. This policy also ensures data is written in unpredictable locations.

These issues are not detrimental enough to avoid using SSDs, and the SSDs' speed benefits are here to stay. As new generations of SSDs come out, these issues become less and less of a meaningful problem. SSD technology is here to stay and grow.

☞ Solid state storage doesn't have to be done on SSDs. For higher performance, high-speed solid-state storage cards can be inserted directly in the computer's extension slots. These cards are expensive, but represent the best choice to host the WORK library due to their speed. For even more speed, RAM can be used. Memory prices now allow hundreds of GB of memory to be reserved as WORK disks.

While SSDs are not yet able to cater to all storage needs, their high speed and their extremely low access times make them obvious options for I/O sensitive applications.

RAID

Another, much older and more common, way to increase performance is to group several disks together and manage them as one volume. This permits running data access queries in parallel as different queries can be sent to different disks, or one query can be split and executed by several disks.

Such a group of disks is called an array, or more generally and more oxymoronically a RAID, or Redundant Array of Inexpensive Disks.

RAID is the common name given to arrays of disks, but is now rather meaningless as the array is not necessarily redundant, nor is it always made of inexpensive disks. RAID arrays normally need all disks included in the array to be of the same size.

Note that RAID arrays can only improve the data transfer rate (throughput) of the storage system. Access time is normally not reduced as disks still need to spin and heads to move to the right location before any data is accessed. Different RAID types, called levels, exist that provide various compromises between retrieval speed, storage capacity and data protection through redundancy.

Three of the mainly used RAID levels are RAID level 0, 1 and 5, and combinations of these. Other raid levels exist but are more rarely used.

Let's have a look at these three RAID array architectures.

RAID 0

RAID level 0 consists in assembling several (at least two) disks into an array and makes this array appear as one big disk that is the sum of the disk spaces.

This configuration provides the greatest boost in speed. When a file is written out, it is split in several parts (one per disk) and these parts are written concurrently on all disks. Likewise, if the file must be read, all disks can read their file part at the same time and send the data back.

The downside of RAID0 is that it offers no redundancy. If one disk dies, the whole volume disappears and all the data is lost. For this reason, this RAID level is only suitable for the work library, where all files are temporary, and only if users can accept some down-time for a failed disk to be replaced when such an event occurs. A RAID0 volume is also called a striped volume.

This configuration has the following characteristics:

- Disk space is high
  All the disks contribute their space
- Reliability is low
  The loss of any one disk triggers the loss of all the data
- Read speed can be very high
  All disks can contribute file parts
- Write speed can be very high
  Write operations can be spread on all disks

Figure 2.1: RAID0 volume. A file is scattered across all the disks

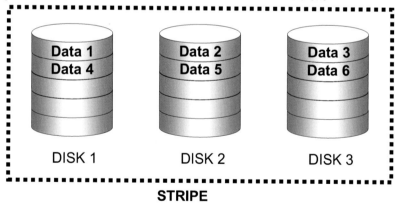

RAID 1

RAID level 1 consists in assembling several disks (usually two) into an array and makes this array appear as one single disk. All the disks are mirroring of each other.

When a file is written out, it is written out in full to all disks at the same time, so there is no speed gain whatsoever there. If a file must be read, all disks can read a different part of the file they hold, so speed gains can be substantial, depending on how smart the RAID controller is.

RAID1 is seldom used with more than 2 disks since only one disk's space is used for data, and all the other disks are used for redundancy.

Because the capacity offered by RAID1 is that of a single disk, RAID1 is also not suitable to create large storage spaces.

This configuration has the following characteristics:

- Disk space is low
  The disk space of only one disk is available
- Reliability is high
  All the disks must die before the data is lost
- Read speed can be very high
  All disks can contribute file parts
- Write speed is low
  Writes have to take place concurrently on all disks

Figure 2.2: RAID1 volume. A file is mirrored on all the disks

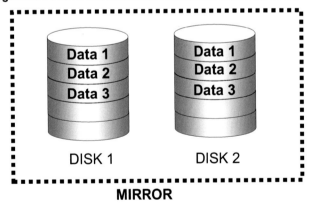

RAID 10

RAID10 is a nested RAID or hybrid RAID.

When using nested RAID levels, some disks are grouped into arrays using a RAID levels, and these disk arrays are then grouped into other arrays.

RAID10 groups disks into mirrors (usually mirror pairs), and nests the mirror groups inside in a stripe. RAID 10 is a stripe of mirrors.

RAID 10 is often used when the redundancy of RAID1 is desired, but a large storage capacity is sought.

This configuration combines the characteristics of RAID1 and RAID0:

- Disk space is low
  Only half of the disk space if used for data, the other half is for redundancy (if the mirrors are pairs of disks)
- Reliability is high
  Any number of disks can die without threatening the RAID10 volume as long as these disks are not in the same mirror.
- If a disk is dead in a 10-disk array and a second disk dies, the chances of then losing the volume are only 1/9.
- Read speed can be very high
  All disks can contribute file parts.
- Write speed can be high
  Writes can be spread across the stripe to each mirror

Figure 2.3: RAID10 volume. A file is mirrored on disk pools, and the mirror pools are striped

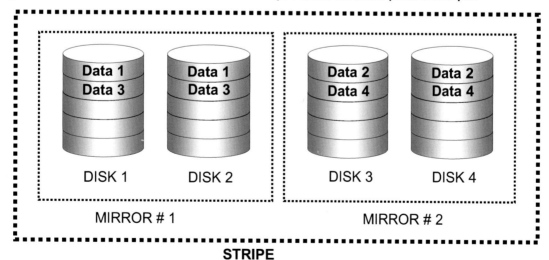

RAID 5

Because RAID1 is so wasteful, since at least half of the space of lost to redundancy, other methods than simply mirroring exist to enable redundancy.

RAID5 uses parity calculations to ensure redundancy and only the space of one disk is lost to redundancy: A block of data on each data disks is read, a parity calculation is performed for this data, and the parity value is written to the parity disk. And so forth for each block of data.

If one disk were to malfunction, its data can be retrieved by reversing the calculation and using the valid data from the remaining disks as well as the parity value to find the original missing data.

To avoid the parity disk becoming a bottleneck when writing data, parity blocks are spread across all the disks. For example, disk1 will hold the parity for the first block of data, but disk2 will hold the parity for the second block, etc.

Sometimes the space of 2 disks is dedicated to the storage of parity. This allows the loss of 2 disks without loss of data. This RAID level is called RAID6.

RAID5 has pros and cons compared to RAID10:

- Disk space is high
  Only the disk space of one disk is lost to redundancy
- Reliability is average
  The loss of any 2 disks triggers the loss of the whole volume and its data. If a disk is dead in a 10-disk array and a second disk dies, the chances of losing the volume are 100%.
- Read speed can be very high
  All disks but one can contribute file parts.
- Write speed is very low
  Each time data is written, parity has to be recalculated and written as well. Each write operation requires to:
  1. Read the old data that is being replaced
  2. Read the old parity
  3. Derive the new parity
  4. Write the new data
  5. Write the new parity
  So one write operation causes four I/O operations. Furthermore, these operations can't happen in any order. The two read operations must be performed before the write operations, which introduces an additional delay.

Note that the write penalty associated with RAID5 is mostly due to the access times required for each of the four I/O operations. The operations themselves are much faster than the time spent waiting for the operations to take place. Because of this, SSDs are not nearly as much a write-speed hindrance as HDDs when used in a RAID5 array. SSDs still suffer from the block-erase limitation and the need to do garbage collection properly, since the OS cannot manage the SSD itself –as it only sees the array, not the disk– by "trimming" it, but in terms of write speed, RAID5 is not nearly as penalising when used with SSDs.

Figure 2.4: RAID5 volume. A file is interleaved with parity data

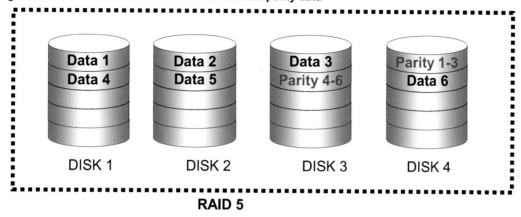

RAID 5

RAID 50

Because RAID5 is fragile (only one disk can be lost before failure) and suffers from a significant write penalty, it is common to nest RAID5 volumes inside RAID0 stripes.

This offers better data protection since one disk in each RAID5 group can die without killing the volume. It also offers better write speed because writes can be spread across all the stripe's RAID5 groups.

Figure 2.5: RAID50 volume. A file is interleaved with parity data in two striped RAID5 pools

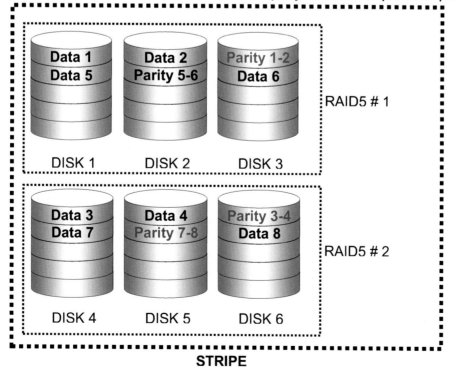

STRIPE

Which hard disk array for SAS data then?

In the SAS world, because IO speed is so important, RAID10 is the most-used method for storing fast permanent data. It is more expensive than RAID5 as half the disk space isn't used for additional data storage, but disk space is cheap and slow SAS jobs are costly. Only in cases when data is seldom refreshed may RAID5 or RAID50 hard disk volumes be an acceptable compromise between cost and speed.

RAID0 can be used for the location of the WORK library. If infrequent process failures are acceptable, RAID0 offers the best speed for the cheapest price. If service continuity is more important than raw speed, RAID10 is the next best option. RAID5 or RAID50 are never an option due to the write penalty.

When using arrays made of SSDs, the recommendations above remain true, but RAID5 is no longer a vastly degraded solution and may be acceptable. As usual, some testing is desirable to find the solution best suited to your data, your processes and your budget.

Spindles

Note that the speed of an array depends on the speed of its constituent disks, but also very much on the number of disks. This is also true if the array uses SSD instead of HDDs.

A 1TB RAID0 volume made of 4x 250GB disks will be faster than a 1TB RAID0 volume made with 2x2 500GB disks if the disks have similar performances. It will also be twice as likely to fail.

A 1TB RAID10 volume made of 4x 250GB disks will also be faster than a 1TB RAID0 volume made with 2x 500GB disks if the disks have similar performance regardless of size. It will not be twice as likely to fail.

☞ When counting disks for the purpose of assessing the number of disks in an array, hence the potential combined speed, IT professionals often refer to them as spindles, as in: "how many spindles in your array?" It will be interesting to see how the terminology evolves when SSD arrays become more common.

Silent data corruption

Just a short note that has nothing to do with performance. People often associate RAID with total data protection. To ensure that data can survive a hardware fault, disks store checksums and RAID arrays (except RAID0) duplicate data. However, these measures are not sufficient to detect all errors, in particular not so-called "bit-rot", especially when the arrays' integrity is not verified ("scrubbed") regularly. Another issue is the "write hole", which can happen if a power failure occurs during a write, and is countered by executing Copy-on-Write. Thankfully these issues are uncommon, but to ensure the best level of protection, a modern file system that also keeps checksums and permits regular scrubs such as ZFS or maybe btrfs is needed. If your data is precious, investigate these issues before this important zip file that you absolutely need can no longer be opened.

Volatile storage (Memory)

SAS jobs typically didn't use to use much memory. It is still common to find SAS sessions limited to 1GB or 512 MB of RAM. This can be justified by the fact that many processes in SAS process bits of data one after another, in a linear manner, and don't use much memory at all.

A typical DATA step will read one or several tables sequentially, may even save some data in arrays for some smart processing across observations and will write out the results sequentially as they are generated. Very little data is used at any time. Likewise, generating list reports or drawing graphics will not consume much memory.

For those processes that can consume memory, like large summarizations or sorts, having more memory is only beneficial if the whole process can fit in memory. As soon as a memory limitation is reached and memory has to be supplemented by utility files on disks, the benefits of any extra memory vanish.

Sorting a 1GB file in 2GB of memory is very fast. On the other hand, sorting this same file in 1GB or memory or in 512MB of memory doesn't make much difference as the data doesn't fit. So increasing the memory available to SAS sessions from say 1GB to 2GB is only beneficial for those tasks loading in memory tables that can fit between these 2 sizes. There is no benefit for smaller tables and no benefit for larger tables either.

Now this is changing. This change is driven by two factors. One factor is that the price of RAM is now so cheap as to be unnoticeable in the overall price of a SAS server or desktop machine. It is possible to buy hundreds of GB of RAM for less than the price of a processor.

Cheap prices would not be very enticing if SAS didn't have ways to use that memory. Of course, traditional tasks like sorting or summarizing or computing statistics can benefit from more memory, and with the incessant growth of data volumes, it looks like this trend will only accelerate. The really interesting gains from more memory don't come from legacy tasks though. Many features of SAS available in version 9 can now take advantage of large amounts of memory, and allow SAS to load substantial amounts of data in memory for faster processing.

These features, like hash tables or in-memory data storage can accelerate SAS processes tremendously. See the section about the possibilities offered by SAS V9's in-memory data processing capabilities, and you can look in the relevant sections to know more about these topics.

These new features will only be available to advanced SAS users who can write programs while keeping performance in mind, and typical point-and-click Enterprise Guide users will not be able to leverage them. On the other hand, if you have advanced SAS programmers in your organization you are in luck: for the cheap price of extra memory, you can speed up your processes tremendously.

How much memory should be made available is of course variable and will depend on the usual factors of what your processes are and what your data is, but considering how cheap RAM is and how expensive slow processes or idle SAS experts are, there is every reason to err on the side of making large quantities of RAM available.

The old adage that SAS processes don't use and don't benefit from vast amounts of memory has been made obsolete and that's a good thing. With memory so cheap, data so plentiful, and SAS embracing in-memory processing, times have never been better to process data!

Processor

This section is potentially the most complex or the simplest of the hardware chapter.

Since I will not go into the complexities of modern CPUs, both because I don't understand all the intricate details and because it would bring no useful information toward the aim of this chapter, I will keep it easy and to-the-point.

I will give a quick overview of some issues surrounding CPUs as a reference, so you can shine at the next geek gathering, but in reality the discussion about CPUs for SAS servers is short and sharp.

The recent evolution of processors

CPUs are evolving much faster than other components and their performance progress apace.

A CPU core's performance depends on two things: how much it can do in one clock cycle, and how fast the clock is.

While the former characteristic (work done by cycle) is slowly increasing, the latter (frequency) isn't.

Whereas CPU speeds used to increase steadily and roughly double every other year, a brutal stalling occurred in the early 2000's when clock frequencies reached 4 GHz. The clock speed of processors hasn't changed much since because of various physical issues, mainly heat output. Instead, CPU manufacturers have opted to add more cores into CPUs. So for new CPU generations, the way to double CPU performance is to double the number of cores rather than to double the clock frequency. In effect, adding more cores is like adding multiple inner-CPUs inside one CPU.

This change in the way CPUs increase their performance has had an arguably negative impact for two reasons:

Usable processing power

When CPUs were merely increasing the speed of their core, a single process could utilise all the CPU's power, provided no other process needed to use the CPU. Adding a faster CPU always meant that the process ran faster. With multiple cores, the single process may use just one core, and the supposedly faster CPU will mostly run idle as other cores remain unused. In order to use all the cores, a process has to be written in a completely different and much more complex manner so that it can run in parallel on several cores. This lack of direct performance improvement is compounded by the fact that synchronising the cores can add significant overhead. So effectively, except for multi-user servers that always run more CPU-intensive processes than they have cores, the growth of usable processing speed for everyday tasks has slowed down.

Software is slowly adapting to this new CPU landscape where processes have to be split across CPUs in order to increase their performance. This is called multi-threading: a process is split into several so-called threads that run concurrently, or in parallel.

In version 9, SAS Institute has enhanced a few procedures and added multi-threading. These procedures can now use multiple CPU cores whenever they are available.

This started with procedures MEANS, REPORT, SORT, SUMMARY, TABULATE and SQL in Base SAS, procedures GLM, LOESS, REG and ROBUSTREG in SAS/STAT, procedure SERVER in SAS/SHARE, procedures DMREG and DMINE in Enterprise Miner, and the SAS Base engine that builds indexes.

In version 9.4, SAS/STAT procedures ADAPTIVEREG, FMM, GLMSELECT, MIXED, QUANTLIFE, QUANTREG, and QUANTSELECT were added to the list.

See the threads section in the Options chapter to know more about using multiple cores or processors with SAS.

Software licensing

Another potential issue with the increase of the number of cores as a way to increase CPU performance has to do with software licensing.

This issue mostly applies to PCs as, in SAS's case at least, bigger systems' licence costs are calculated on a CPU-processing-power basis. On PCs by contrast, when CPUs increased their speed by 50% from a clock frequency of say 2 GHz to a frequency of 3 GHz, users paid the same software licencing price, which depended only on the number of CPUs. Licences were paid on a per-CPU basis and increase in CPU power was just part of the natural evolution of technology.

Nowadays, clock frequencies don't change. Instead, the number of cores changes. At the same time, software vendors, SAS included, have moved from a licence price based on the number of CPUs to a licence price based on the number of cores in the machine. So when you upgrade your machine from a 4-core CPU to a 6-core CPU, your licence price may well increase even though you may only be following the normal evolution of technology.

To be fair, SAS Institute has been more lenient than some, and has tried to take into account the change in CPU technology by changing their licensing conditions. As I write, the first-tier licence covers CPUs containing one to four cores, which seems reasonable. The issue of software licensing can nonetheless have potentially expensive consequences.

Caching

Being the fastest-clocked components in a computer, CPUs have the most sophisticated caching mechanisms. Today's CPUs have several layered levels of caches (3 usually), with level 1 being the smallest and fastest, then level 2 being larger and slower, and then level 3 which is even larger and slower. If the L3 cache cannot be used, the CPU will then access the main memory. We'll never have to worry about this type of technological detail when using SAS, but this highlights how important caching is to the performance of processes. More on caching later.

Wimpy vs. Brawny

As for caching, I only mention this topic in passing and we won't go into the details. There is an interesting debate - interesting for the technology-inclined at least - among people who run vast numbers of processes: is it better to have many cheap low-power low-heat CPUs, or is it better to have fewer high-performance CPUs, or a combination? High-performance CPUs can complete one process faster, but when you have many processes, maybe it is the average processing time over all the processes that matters. I'll leave this debate here as it doesn't really concern SAS servers. You can read more on the web if you are interested in knowing more and want to know if wimpy is better than brawny.

CPUs for running SAS

Having squandered time reading CPU factoids, erm I mean having read some background information about what's happening in the CPU world, you'll be glad to know that things are rather simple regarding SAS and processors, at least on PC platforms. The main limiting factor is the price of your SAS licence price. CPUs are cheap in comparison. You have to define which licence price bracket your machine load puts you in. And then you should install the maximum number of cores allowed by the licence. The CPU of choice should be the CPU that gives you the most processing power per core.

As an example, let's suppose that your needs put you in the 5-to-12 core SAS licence bracket. You then have the choice of using say one 12-core CPU or two 6-core CPUs or three 4-core CPUs or six 2-core CPUs. You need to look at the benchmarks and select the CPUs that offer the highest per-core performance. That's the optimal way to get a good return on your SAS licence investment. So if a 6-core CPU is 30% faster[1] than a 4-core CPU, the 4-core model should be used: the 6-core CPU matches the per-core performance of the 4-core CPU only if it is 50% faster. If the core performance figures are close, fewer CPUs with more cores each are to be preferred for two reasons:

- The cores are closer to each other and can benefit from faster communication with each other,
- The hardware cost will probably be lower, both for the CPU cost and for the motherboard cost if fewer CPU sockets are needed.

These basic guidelines should keep you in the right ball park when making a purchase decision.

---

[1] Faster means having more processing power, not having a faster clock

Caching

The operating system file cache is a temporary storage area in main memory used to retain data that is written to and read from disk. Any memory not used by the operating system or by applications can be used as file cache memory, and the operating system usually makes I/O operations go through the file cache. The idea behind it is to lower the number of physical disk I/Os, which is desirable because disks are slower than memory. The main reason for this slowness is latency, which I covered above. Using the file cache improves I/O performance because it uses techniques called write-behinds, read-aheads, fast writes and fast reads.

Write-behinds (also called lazy writes) are done when disk updates are not done immediately, but written "lazily" later on. The assumption is that an application writing a bit of data to a portion of a file will probably write multiple times to the same file portion, but these multiples writes will take place in memory and physical update on disk will take place only once.

Read-aheads use a similar principle, i.e. the assumption is that when an application reads a portion of a file, it will likely want to next portion very soon. So the caching mechanism reads some data before the data is requested, which takes very little time because it is already reading data at the same location.

Fast reads are simply the consequence of the read-aheads, where the application gets much faster performance because the requested data comes directly from memory instead of coming from the physical disk. Another case of fast read is when the same data is requested more than once, and the later reads can be retrieved from the cache rather than from disk. Fast writes are similar: writing to memory is faster than waiting for disks to be in the right position before writing to them.

☞ When the operating system finds data already in memory, this is called a cache hit, and this allows fast reads to occur. Conversely, when the operating system cannot find the requested data in memory and has to access the disk, this is called a cache miss.

☞ The main benefit of caching comes from avoiding the access time delays. Since SSDs have much reduced access times, caching is less beneficial when using SSDs. On one hand, RAM is much faster than the Flash memory used in SSDs, but on the other hand caching does have costly overheads. So caching SSDs is not always as obvious a decision as it can be for hard disks.

While caching works well and speeds up jobs most of the time, we will see when looking at Direct Input/Output options that caching is not always desirable, and that there are cases when caching is undesirable.

It's all about compromise

Seeking best performance is a balancing act. In this book, we seek lower elapse times, but there may be other priorities. Some systems are invoiced by CPU time, and on those systems the lowest possible CPU time might be the desired outcome.

Generally speaking, decreasing or increasing the availability of some resources can have an impact on other resources. We illustrate below how compromises are made by representing a computer's main resources and some common trade-offs. Other resources, such as network link loads, are not on this diagram.

① When data is stored in a compressed form, the required disk space is lower and the number of I/O operations decreases, but on-the-fly data compression and decompression increases the CPU load.

② If a process (a sort for example) cannot be completed in memory, SAS starts paging the process and this greatly increases disk load and elapse time. It also increases CPU usage ④.

③ When sufficient memory is available, disk caching can reduce the load on the disk. When even more memory is available, tables can be loaded permanently in memory.

Figure 2.6: Reducing the load on one resource often increases the load on another resource

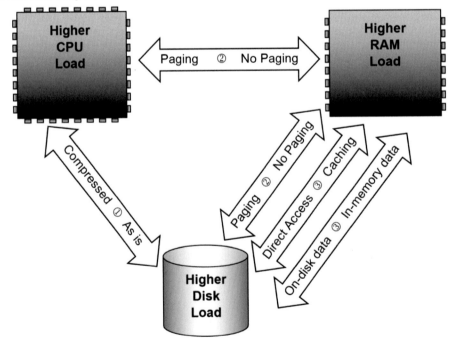

Keep these trade-offs in mind. There are more of course. For example, storing short code values and formatting them into long labels saves space, but requires CPU time. Storing calculated values rather than deriving them as needed conserves CPU at the expense of space. It's all a matter of choice. In the SAS world, while the licensing is based on the CPUs, the slowest resource is often the disk, so that's generally the resource we try to spare.

What to remember when building a SAS server

If you haven't read this chapter, or if this is too much information to assimilate at once, here is what to remember: SAS is most often limited by the speed of its access to data. So when provisioning a SAS server, the main thing is generally to ensure fast access to data. That's where money should be spent. Large arrays of fast disks in the form of Direct-Attached Storage (DAS), solid state storage in the form of SSDs or slot-in cards, RAM disks for the work libraries, will return worthwhile speed improvements.

This is true whether the server is on dedicated physical hardware, or virtual in a VM, or hosted on the cloud. SAS jobs often involve moving a lot of data, and any speed improvement in this area helps.

This is good news because SAS licences are based on the number of CPUs. So adding more memory and faster storage is free from a licensing view point.

The goal is to constantly keep your CPUs busy rather than waiting. If you do this, you have a balanced server in terms of resource utilisation, and have built the best server for your licensing budget.

Summary

An overview has been given of what components affect SAS performance, how these components function, and how they interact with each other.

This knowledge will be used to understand how SAS makes use of these components and what part of a computer the various SAS options affect.

More importantly and aligned with this book's goal, this knowledge is supplied as a background to understand why some SAS option settings can be detrimental while other settings are beneficial, depending on the conditions.

Chapter 2

Hardware: what is performance?

Chapter 3

Common-sense Ways to Improve Performance

Introduction

Many readers might already know about the points mentioned in this chapter. On the other hand, many less-seasoned SAS users will learn a few things that they should know before reading about more advanced topics. To those readers who find the following points obvious or common-place, I apologise. I just couldn't write a book about performance and leave out these fundamental points. They represent to vast majority of low-hanging, high-benefit fruity enhancements one can make to SAS programs, and they are still essential to the foundation knowledge of SAS programmers.

Reminders

Create SAS data sets instead of accessing flat text files.

SAS uses a number of optimisation techniques to speed up access to data stored in SAS format, so do store your data in SAS tables. You can easily export it when needed.

Subsetting

One very effective way to decrease run time is to reduce the number of observations processed. The main ways of doing this are the WHERE and the IF statements.

Use a WHERE statement rather than an IF statement

The WHERE statement is processed as the data is being read. If the data doesn't match the WHERE clause criteria, it is discarded before being loaded into the PDV for processing. That's the earliest possible time to discard it, so that's good.

Another reason to use a WHERE statement is that it can make use of what is known about the data sets, like indexes or sorting order.

Here is our data sample, with 5 million observations.

```
data T5E6(compress=no);
  A='aaaaaa';
  do I=1 to 5e6;
    output;
  end;
run;
```

First we subset with a WHERE clause.

```
data _null_;
  set T5E6;
  where I<100;
run;
```

Note that only 99 observations are loaded for processing by the DATA step.

```
NOTE: There were 99 observations read from the data set WORK.T5E6.
      WHERE I<100;
NOTE: DATA statement used (Total process time):
      real time           3.87 seconds
```

Then we subset with an IF clause.

```
data _null_;
  set T5E6;
  if I<100;
run;
```

All observations are seen by the DATA step and processed. They are loaded in the PDV and then discarded when the IF statement returns FALSE.

```
NOTE: There were 5000000 observations read from the data set WORK.T5E6.
NOTE: DATA statement used (Total process time):
      real time           3.98 seconds
```

☞ WHERE statements are faster than IF statements when values are simply compared.

☞ WHERE statements can only by subset using variables present in the data sets.

☞ If the data sets have different variables used for subsetting, you can use WHERE data set options rather than IF statement, like:

```
merge CUSTOMERS (in=RET where=(CUS_TYPE='RETAIL'))
      BALANCES  (in=DTE where=(MSMT_DTE='01JAN2013'd));
by CUS_ID;
if RET and DTE;
```

instead of :

```
merge CUSTOMERS
      BALANCES  ;
by CUS_ID;
if CUS_TYPE='RETAIL' and MSMT_DTE='01JAN2013'd;
```

Use an IF statement rather than a WHERE statement

Yes, I know, I just told you the opposite. As usual rules are not universal, and the final rule is: it depends. WHERE statements are usually much faster than IF statements for testing straight equalities or inequalities. When functions are used, this is no longer the case.

```data _null_; set T5E6; where round(I)<100; run; ```	NOTE: DATA statement used (Total process time): real time 13.45 seconds
```data _null_; set T5E6; if round(I)<100; run; ```	NOTE: DATA statement used (Total process time): real time 6.21 seconds

When we use a function, WHERE clause evaluation times soar. SAS functions are optimised to read data from the PDV, and having a WHERE clause seems to cause some inefficiencies.

☞ IF statements are faster than WHERE statements when functions are used.

Make use of data organisation

Let's keep the same example, but add some metadata or an index so that SAS has more information about the data set.

Example 1: Data is sorted but not validated.

First, we set the SORTEDBY flag.

```
data T5E6(sortedby=I);
  do I=1 to 5e6;
    output;
  end;
run;
data _null_ ;
  set T5E6;
  where I<100;
run;
```

No difference here with the previous use of the where clause:
no optimisation has taken place:

```
NOTE: There were 99 observations read from the data set WORK.T5E6.
      WHERE I<100;
NOTE: DATA statement used (Total process time):
      real time          3.89 seconds
```

Example 2: Data is sorted and validated

If we validate the sort, or if we index the data set, the WHERE clause will use this information to optimise the processing.

```
proc sort data=T5E6 out=T5E6(index=(I)) presorted; Sort & index;
  by I;
run;

data _null_;
  set T5E6;
  where I<100;              * Index is used for optimisation;
run;

data _null_;
  set T5E6(idxwhere=no); * Sort order is used for optimisation;
  where I<100;
run;
```

When the data is sorted and validated, run time for our example is reduced to nothing regardless of whether we use an index or the sort order:

```
INFO: Index I selected for WHERE clause optimization.
      real time            0.01 seconds
...
INFO: Data set option (IDXWHERE=NO) forced a sequential pass of the data rather than use
of an index for where-clause processing.
      real time            0.01 seconds
```

☞ The IF clause will not take advantage of sorted data or indexes.

Subset as early as possible

When you have to use an IF statement to subset observations, do it as early as possible so you can skip to the next observation right away if the values don't match the selection criteria.
There is no need to process data that will be discarded.

Here we subset data that is not common to both tables using WHERE options, which are individual to each table. Then right after the data is read, we further subset before doing any further processing.

```
  merge PAYMENTS (keep=CUS_ID PAYMT_DTE where=(CUS_TYPE='RETAIL'))
        BALANCES (keep=CUS_ID MSMT_DTE );
  by CUS_ID;
  if PAYMT_DTE < MSMT_DTE;
...more code comes after
```

Conditional processing

If your tests are repeated a very high number of times, you may want to measure the efficiency of the various test syntaxes applicable to your case. While some syntaxes do require more resources, in the real world this seldom matters. The worst syntax in my examples runs 5 billion tests 80 seconds. That's 5 million tests in 0.08s. So unless you have a really huge number of tests to run, code legibility is probably what matters the most in my opinion. Here are examples.

Example 1: Series of IF tests, all test conditions are assessed.

```data _null_ ; do I=1 to 1e9; if I <= 2e8 then A=1; if 2e8 < I <= 4e8 then A=2; if 4e8 < I <= 6e8 then A=3; if 6e8 < I <= 8e8 then A=4; if 8e8 < I <=10e8 then A=5; end; run;```	real time 17.98 seconds

Example 2: Series of IF / ELSE tests, test conditions stop being assessed as soon as a condition is met. This is more efficient.

```data _null_ ; do I=1 to 1e9; if I <= 2e8 then A=1; else if I <= 4e8 then A=2; else if I <= 6e8 then A=3; else if I <= 8e8 then A=4; else if I <=10e8 then A=5; end; run;```	real time 11.65 seconds

Example 3: Series of tests using the SELECT statement.

This syntax's efficiency is similar, slightly lower maybe, to that of the previous example.

```data _null_ ; do I=1 to 1e9; select; when(I <= 2e8) A=1; when(I <= 4e8) A=2; when(I <= 6e8) A=3; when(I <= 8e8) A=4; when(I <=10e8) A=5; otherwise; end; end; run;```	real time 11.94 seconds

Example 4: The IFN() and IFC() functions are much less efficient than IF tests.

Although I am sometimes performance-obsessed, this has paradoxically become my favourite syntax when assigning a value to a variable because I find it the most legible.

I hope SAS will make these functions smarter and more efficient one day: As for all functions. SAS derives the values of all the function's parameters.

Obviously and by design, there is no need for these two functions to test all conditions and to derive all result values all the time.

```data _null_ ; do I=1 to 1e9; A = ifn(I <= 2e8, 1 ,ifn(I <= 4e8, 2 ,ifn(I <= 6e8, 3 ,ifn(I <= 8e8, 4 ,ifn(I <=10e8, 5 , .)))))); end; run; ```	real time 1:21.88

Example 5: Boolean multiplier.

The following syntax is sometimes used when creating complex formulas, in statistical models for example. This syntax is rather inefficient, but has the advantage of compacity and clarity when many conditions have to be tested in order to derive a value. It is often used to assign scores when applying a decision-tree-like model.

```data _null_; do I=1 to 1e9; A=(I <= 2e8) * 1 +(2e8 < I <= 4e8) * 2 +(4e8 < I <= 6e8) * 3 +(6e8 < I <= 8e8) * 4 +(8e8 < I <=10e8) * 5; end; run; ```	real time 51.98 seconds

Note that the parts in brackets are tests. They return a Boolean value of 0 or 1 to the arithmetic calculator. By using this syntax, where tests are embedded in calculations, many tests can be carried on the fly while building a formula. When a test fails, the expression attached to the test is nullified, and when it succeeds, the expression is added to the formula.

CLASS vs. BY

Along with "WHERE is better than IF", a very common truism when using procedures that include the classify variables is "BY is better than CLASS." This makes sense, right? If the data set is sorted, let the procedure know about it and reduce the amount of processing.

This is not always true however. A BY statement involves splitting the process into smaller successive chunks, and this can be detrimental to the overall performance. This is especially true since SAS version 9 introduced multi-threading.

Here is an example of the impact of these statements

```
data TEST;
  do I=1 to 1e3;
   do J=1 to 1e3;
    output;
   end;
  end;
run;

sasfile TEST load;

proc summary data=TEST;
  class I J;
 output out=SUM;
run;

proc summary data=TEST;
  by I J;
 output out=SUM;
run;

sasfile TEST close;
```

```
NOTE: Multiple concurrent threads will be used to
summarize data.
NOTE: PROCEDURE SUMMARY used (Total process time):
      real time          1.36 seconds
      user cpu time      1.82 seconds
      system cpu time    0.11 seconds
      memory             92290.43k
      OS Memory          138752.00k

NOTE: PROCEDURE SUMMARY used (Total process time):
      real time          6.06 seconds
      user cpu time      2.39 seconds
      system cpu time    3.48 seconds
      memory             1778.56k
      OS Memory          49232.00k
```

As you can see, there are several differences in the way resources are used.

Table 3.1: Comparison of resource utilisation

Resource	BY Statement	CLASS Statement
Real time	✗ The procedure takes longer to complete the task	✓ Because multiple threads are used, the procedure completes sooner
CPU Time	✗ More CPU time is needed	✓ Less CPU time is needed
Memory	✓ Less memory is needed	✗ Much more memory is needed

☞ Never sort a table just to call one of these procedures. A CLASS statement will always be much faster than calling PROC SORT. The only valid reason to sort is if the procedure can't complete successfully due to lack of memory.

Testing strings for equality

By default, when two strings are compared, the longest string dictates how many characters will be evaluated. SAS pads the shorter string with spaces to the length of the longer string before making the comparison. This has a significant impact on performance as you can see below.

| ```
* Takes 1.8 seconds;
data _null_;
  length A $16 B $160;
  do I=1 to 1e8;
    if A=B;
  end;
run;
``` |

| ```
* Takes 0.3 seconds;
data _null_;
  length A $16 B $16;
  do I=1 to 1e8;
    if A=B;
  end;
run;
``` |

Variable lengths are usually set, and we cannot change this parameter. However, if appropriate, we can choose to compare only the meaningful parts of the strings.

This is done by using the =: operator instead of the = operator. The colon modifier after the operator makes SAS truncate the longer string to the length of the shorter string, instead of padding the short string.

⏃ **Danger: I do not recommend that you use this technique without due care as the strings are not fully compared. I mostly mention this behaviour for completeness, and to tickle your performance radar.**

| ```
* Colon modifier;
* Takes 0.8 seconds;
data _null_;
  length A $1600;
  A='abc';
  do I=1 to 1e8;
    if A=:'abc';
  end;
run;
``` | ```
* No colon modifier;
* Takes 11 seconds;
data _null_;
  length A $1600;
  A='abc';
  do I=1 to 1e8;
    if A='abc';
  end;
run;
``` | ```
* Shorter string;
* Takes 2 seconds;
data _null_;
  length A $160;
  A='abc';
  do I=1 to 1e8;
    if A=:'abc';
  end;
run;
``` |
```

Use faster functions

There are often many ways to perform a task, and they are seldom equivalent from a performance viewpoint. When that's the case, be aware of the efficiency of various methods.

Example 1: Search a string.

```
options nofullstimer compress=no source;
data T;
  A='aaaaaaaaaaaaaaaaa';
  do I=1 to 5e7;
    output;
  end;
run;
sasfile T1E8 load;

data _null_; set T; where A like    '%a%'; run;
data _null_; set T; where A contains 'a'; run;
data _null_; set T; where   index(A,'a'); run;
data _null_; set T; if      index(A,'a'); run;
data _null_; set T; if       find (A,'a'); run;
data _null_; set T; if compress(A,'a','k')='a';run;
data _null_; set T; if prxmatch('/a/',A); run;
```

real time   7.84 seconds
real time   7.17 seconds
real time   11.16 seconds
real time   2.81 seconds
real time   2.96 seconds
real time   13.03 seconds
real time   11.10 seconds

The WHERE clause struggles again, and the old and simple INDEX function wins the day. The WHERE-specific operators LIKE and CONTAINS are slower than IF and INDEX.

Example 2: Search a string, case insensitive

```
where A like     '%A%' or A like    '%a%';
where A contains 'A'   or A contains 'a';
where index(A,'A')     or index(A,'a');
if    index(A,'A')     or index(A,'a');
if    find (A,'a','i');
if compress(A,'aA','k') ne ' ';
if compress(A,'a','ki') ne ' ';
if prxmatch('/[aA]/',A) ;
if prxmatch('/a/i',A);
```

12.69 seconds
10.03 seconds
18.22 seconds
3.97 seconds
3.40 seconds
12.38 seconds
13.32 seconds
12.55 seconds
12.57 seconds

The newer FIND function shows the usefulness of its extra parameters

Example 3: Test a string's first character.

```
data _null_; set T; where A          like 'a%'; run;
data _null_; set T; where A             =:'a'; run;
data _null_; set T; if A                =:'a'; run;
data _null_; set T; if index(A,'a')     = 1  ; run;
data _null_; set T; if put(A,$1.)       = 'a'; run;
data _null_; set T; if first(A)         = 'a'; run;
data _null_; set T; if substr(A,1,1)    = 'a'; run;
data _null_; set T; if prxmatch('/^a/',A)    ; run;
```

8.28 seconds
7.63 seconds
2.25 seconds
2.74 seconds
2.99 seconds
2.84 seconds
3.92 seconds
13.55 seconds

The INDEX function is again performing well, but the =: operator, which only processes the start of strings, is best for this test.

Careful with those intervals!

Several syntaxes exist to check if a number falls within an interval, but all syntaxes are not created equal. In fact, they don't even all do the same thing.

Speed

Here is our test: We create a long narrow file of integers. Then we select values between 1 and 4 using seven different syntaxes.

To keep I/Os out of the equation, we load the file in memory first.

```
data T1E8;
  length X 3;
  do X=1 to 1e8;
    output;
  end;
run;
sasfile T load;
data T1; set T1E8; where 1<=X<=4          ;
data T2; set T1E8; where X in (1,2,3,4)    ;
data T3; set T1E8; where X between 1 and 4 ;
data T4; set T1E8; where X in (1:4)        ;
data T5; set T1E8; if    1<=X<=4           ;
data T6; set T1E8; if    X in (1,2,3,4)    ;
data T7; set T1E8; if    X in (1:4)        ;
run;
sasfile T close;
```

Only the first 4 observations will be kept. Here are the results:

where 1<=X<=4 ;	real time	7.27 seconds
where X in (1,2,3,4) ;	real time	7.17 seconds
where X between 1 and 4 ;	real time	7.11 seconds
where X in (1:4) ;	real time	26.61 seconds
if 1<=X<=4 ;	real time	5.94 seconds
if X in (1,2,3,4) ;	real time	8.13 seconds
if X in (1:4) ;	real time	8.35 seconds

Five out of seven syntaxes run in 7 to 8 seconds, and as expected IF tests take longer to run than WHERE clauses. Two syntaxes stand out, one being fast, one being slow.

The 2 extremes are:

- The fastest run is an IF test at less than 6 seconds. I don't know why this test should be faster than a similar where clause. Something to look into....
- The slowest run is a huge 26 seconds. Let's have a closer look at this run. This run's log displays an interesting message:

```
WHERE (X=INT(X)) and (X>=1 and X<=4);
```

Wait. What?

That's why it takes so long: This run calls the INT() function.

So beware of the IN operator using a range in a WHERE clause: it is very slow.

Logic

Let's do another series of tests. Not for speed this time, but for results.

We want to make sure we subset what we want, so we use 20 decimal numbers this time, and the very same subsets. Let's see what happens.

```
data T;
  do X=1 to 10 by .5;
    output;
  end;
run;
data T1; set T; where 1<=X<=4            ;
data T2; set T; where X in (1,2,3,4)     ;
data T3; set T; where X between 1 and 4 ;
data T4; set T; where X in (1:4)         ;
data T5; set T; if    1<=X<=4            ;
data T6; set T; if    X in (1,2,3,4)     ;
data T7; set T; if    X in (1:4)         ;
run;
```

How many records are we going to keep in your opinion?

Are all these filters going to yield the same results?

```
where 1<=X<=4            ;        The data set WORK.T1 has 7 observations
where X in (1,2,3,4)     ;        The data set WORK.T2 has 4 observations
where X between 1 and 4 ;         The data set WORK.T3 has 7 observations
where X in (1:4)         ;        The data set WORK.T4 has 4 observations
if    1<=X<=4            ;        The data set WORK.T5 has 7 observations
if    X in (1,2,3,4)     ;        The data set WORK.T6 has 4 observations
if    X in (1:4)         ;        The data set WORK.T7 has 4 observations
```

Not all syntaxes are equivalent, but you knew this, right? The IN operator only checks for integers.

The `if X in (1:4)` and `where X in (1:4)` syntaxes yield the same result: they both check for integer values, but there is something not quite right with the speed of `where X in (1:4)` as we've seen above, so avoid it.

Only keep the variables you need

Only keep the variables you need for subsequent steps in your DATA step.

To do this, make use of the DROP and KEEP statements to shed unwanted variables from the output, but also make sure to use the DROP= and KEEP= data set option to only read the data you need.

For example, here we only read the useful sales data, and only output the data used for graphing.

```
data GRAPH1;
  set ALL_MONTHLY_SALES_DATA(keep=MONTH NAME AMOUNT3);
  keep MONTH HTML PLOT_AMOUNT;
... more processing to prepare the graph data
run;
proc gchart data=GRAPH1;
  vbar MONTH/sumvar=PLOT_AMOUNT html=HTML;
run;
quit;
```

☞ Make sure you only keep needed variables when reading data.

If you only use the KEEP statement, all variables are read; Only the variables in the KEEP statement are output, but all variables are read.

By using the KEEP= option on the input data set, only needed data is read.

☞ Together with subsetting unwanted data, keeping only the variables you need is one of the simplest and most effective ways to speed up your code when you process large tables.

☞ Using KEEP rather than DROP allows to keep track of what the code does and how the data flows.

Make arrays faster

If you want to get the best speed out of arrays, there are two things to consider beyond the obvious like dimensioning the array correctly.

When using arrays, make them _TEMPORARY_ if possible.

Temporary arrays elements are not dataset variables: they don't exist in the Program Data Vector (PDV). This saves a lot of retrieval and management time, but means that they don't have variable names and must be referred to by the array name and dimension index. They also are not reset to missing at the end of the implicit DATA step loop iteration, but rather are retained, thus resulting in even less processing.

All this optimises retrieval and management time.

Note how much more time and memory is required to create the second array:

<table>
<tr><td>

```
data _null_;
  array A[1500,1500] 8 _TEMPORARY_;
run;
```

</td><td>

real time	0.02 seconds
user cpu time	0.02 seconds
system cpu time	0.01 seconds
memory	17725.33k
OS Memory	32548.00k

</td></tr>
<tr><td>

```
data _null_;
  array A[1500,1500] 8 ;
run;
```

</td><td>

real time	11.38 seconds
user cpu time	11.07 seconds
system cpu time	0.30 seconds
memory	324038.92k
OS Memory	348284.00k

</td></tr>
</table>

We can see below that temporary arrays elements are not dataset variables:

<table>
<tr><td>

```
data _null_;
  array A[5] 8 _TEMPORARY_;
  array B[5] 8 ;
  put _ALL_;
run;
```

</td><td>

B1=. B2=. B3=. B4=. B5=. _ERROR_=0 _N_=1

</td></tr>
</table>

Iterate array elements in sequential order

When elements of an array are read sequentially, memory can be accessed in a predictable manner, and memory cache mechanisms can optimise this access. Memory caches are often built into the architecture of microprocessors nowadays, and rely on the same block of data being accessed several times. So when you read the first element of an array, the subsequent elements will be read too, and cached. This means that when the second element is accessed by the processor, it will already be available from the processor cache.

For this caching mechanism to work, the data access has to be sequential. That's easy enough to do when the SAS array is mono-dimensional, but in the case of multi-dimensional arrays, care must be taken. Multi-dimensional SAS arrays are simply mono-dimensional arrays with a fancy indexing mechanism. This can be seen here:

<table>
<tr><td>

```
data _null_;
  array A[3,2] (1,2,3,4,5,6);
  do X=1 to 3;
    do Y=1 to 2;
      put X= Y= A[X,Y]=;
    end;
  end;
run;
```

</td><td>

```
X=1 Y=1 A1=1
X=1 Y=2 A2=2
X=2 Y=1 A3=3
X=2 Y=2 A4=4
X=3 Y=1 A5=5
X=3 Y=2 A6=6
```

</td></tr>
</table>

In this multi-dimensional array, by looping through the first dimension, then through the second dimension, we are accessing a mono-dimensional array sequentially as seen in the third column. If the inner loop was using X and the outer loop was using Y, we would not be accessing the array sequentially.

Let's see if that makes a difference.
Here we have an array with 1500x1500 elements, and we scan it 100 times.

The first scan is done sequentially (X in the outer loop), the second one isn't.

```
%macro test;
   %do i=1 %to 2;
      %if &i=1 %then %let order=X,Y;       Order= X,Y
      %else          %let order=Y,X;
      data _null_;                            real time         7.61 seconds
        put "Order= &order";                  user cpu time     7.59 seconds
        array A [1500,1500] 8                 system cpu time   0.00 seconds
             _TEMPORARY_;
        do RUN=1 to 100;
           do X=1 to 1500;                  Order= Y,X
              do Y=1 to 1500;
                 A[&order.]=1;                 real time        19.11 seconds
              end;                            user cpu time     19.05 seconds
           end;                               system cpu time   0.01 seconds
        end;
     run;
  %end;
%mend; %test;
```

Accessing the array in the right order is more than twice as fast.

This is not a ground-shattering loss of speed for most applications, but if you make heavy use of arrays, you may want to keep this in mind.

Numeric variable length

If you are interested in performance, you know that the LENGTH statement allows you to shorten the data set space occupied by numeric variables, at the possible cost of precision loss if you use this option inappropriately. But there is more to know.

The PDV does it its way

Did you know that the PDV always uses the full 8 bytes for numbers? And did you know that a bit of CPU time is needed to expand the shortened number to its full 8-byte length in the PDV?

The CPU cost is minuscule for most applications, and the I/O benefits of a reduced length normally outweigh this, but there may be cases where this matters.

The PDV is not affected by numeric variable length as seen here:

```
data T;
  length I 3;
  I=22222;     put '1- ' i=;        1- I=22222
data _null_;
  set T;       put '2- ' i=;        2- I=22220
  I=22222;     put '3- ' i=;        3- I=22222
run;
```

Benefits of shortening a numeric field

Even when variable lengths have been reduced, it is still possible to further compress data. The numbers' binary values contain repeated bits that can be taken advantage of using the COMPRESS option, especially if the observations are long. See the COMPRESS option for more information on reducing record length while increasing CPU usage.

Here are 4 examples using numeric variables, where we try combinations of shortening and compressing the data. As usual, it is best that you try various options with your own data.

Example 1: Full variable length; No observation compression.

```
data T;
   array var [99] 8;
   do i=1 to 99;  var[i]=i*9; end;*fill array;
   do i=1 to 1e6; output;     end;*fill table;
   stop;
run;
```

File size: 781.3 MB

real time   13.78 seconds
user cpu time   0.61 seconds
system cpu time 1.74 seconds

Example 2: Reduced variable length; No observation compression.
File size and elapse time are halved.

```
data T;
   array var [99] 4;
   do i=1 to 99;  var[i]=i*9; end;*fill array;
   do i=1 to 1e6; output;     end;*fill table;
   stop;
run;
```

File size: 390.6 MB

real time   5.84 seconds
user cpu time   0.40 seconds
system cpu time 0.96 seconds

Example 3: Full variable length; Binary observation compression.
File size reduced further, CPU usage increases.

```
data T(compress=binary);
   array var [99] 8;
   do i=1 to 99;  var[i]=i*9; end;*fill array;
   do i=1 to 1e6; output;     end;*fill table;
   stop;
run;
```

File size: 332.7 MB

real time   9.97 seconds
user cpu time   6.97 seconds
system cpu time 0.63 seconds

Example 4: Reduced variable length; Binary observation compression.
File size similar to example3, CPU usage slightly better.

```
data T(compress=binary);
   array var [99] 4;
   do i=1 to 99;  var[i]=i*9; end;*fill array;
   do i=1 to 1e6; output;     end;*fill table;
   stop;
run;
```

File size: 332.7 MB

real time   9.66 seconds
user cpu time   6.15 seconds
system cpu time 0.60 seconds

Which way you store data depends on your circumstances, but it is often possible to improve performance if your data is suitable.

Other facts about shortened numeric fields

As a reminder, here is the list by variable length and platform of the largest integer absolute values that can be represented exactly. Precision can be lost if this not respected.

Variable Length (bytes)	IBM Mainframe		IEEE (Unix & PC)	
	Largest exact integer		**Largest exact integer**	
2	256	(2^8)	N/A	
3	65,536	(2^{16})	8,192	(2^{13})
4	16,777,216	(2^{24})	2,097,152	(2^{21})
5	4,294,967,296	(2^{32})	536,870,912	(2^{29})
6	1,099,511,627,776	(2^{40})	137,438,953,472	(2^{37})
7	281,474,946,710,65	(2^{48})	35,184,372,088,832	(2^{45})
8	72,057,594,037,927,936	(2^{56})	9,007,199,254,740,992	(2^{53})
8	**Largest possible number: 7.2E75 $\approx 2^{252}$**		**Largest possible number: 1.8E308 $\approx 2^{1024}$**	

☞ As a second reminder, decimal numbers should always be stored in full-length 8-byte fields.

☞ Note that for a given length, the values on each line are not the largest integers possibly represented. As you saw in the "Careful with those intervals!" section, we can store much larger numbers than the above limits. But larger numbers will be rounded down to the nearest binary value available for the chosen variable length.

☞ This is possible because numbers are stored in two parts: the mantissa, which gives the precision, and the exponent, which basically shifts the decimal dot. When the length of a numeric field is shortened, only the mantissa bits are trimmed. Since the exponent bits are untouched, the largest possible number is essentially the same regardless of variable length.

☞ Out of the 64 bits (8 bytes) SAS uses to store numbers, IBM systems use more bits for the mantissa, and fewer bits for the exponent than IEEE systems. That's why IBM mainframes can store larger exact integers, but the largest possible number is smaller. And vice-versa for ASCII systems.

☞ When copying data between systems, you may lose information. If you copy from an IBM mainframe, you may lose exact digits. Conversely, if you copy a number greater than 7.2E75 to an IBM mainframe, it will be stored as 7.2E75.

☞ If you want to know more about this topic, there exists numerous documents and papers that delve into the details and intricacies of SAS number storage for your mathematical enlightenment.

Avoid multiple passes through data

This section is bound to look simplistic, but I cannot avoid this obvious piece of recommendation. When you read or process data, plan carefully and do everything that needs being done in one go. I can't remember all the times I have seen successive steps that could be grouped into one.

Consider the following example, which is totally made up, but sadly, realistic.

```
data T1;          * Subset 1;
  set T5E6;                        NOTE: DATA statement used
  where I<5e5;                           real time      22.27 seconds
data T2;          * Only keep I;
  set T1;                          NOTE: DATA statement used
  keep I;                                real time      16.13 seconds
data T3;          * Derive J;
  set T2;                          NOTE: DATA statement used
  J= mod(I,4);                           real time       0.66 seconds
proc sort data=T3 out=T4;
  by descending I;                 NOTE: PROCEDURE SORT used
  where J;      * Subset 2 & sort;       real time       1.30 seconds
data T5;
  set T4;                          NOTE: DATA statement used
  if lag(I)<50; * Subset 3;              real time       0.50 seconds
run;
```

This can easily be re-written as:

```
proc sort data=T5E6(keep=I)
        out =T1;* Sort;           NOTE: PROCEDURE SORT used
  where I<5e5;    * Subset & keep;      real time      16.60 seconds
  by descending I;
data T2;                          NOTE: DATA statement used
  set T1;                               real time       0.57 seconds
  J= mod(I,4);     * Derive J;
  if J;            * Subset 2;
  if lag(I)<50;    * Subset 3;
run;
```

Reducing the number of steps yielded great gains.

We can also subset earlier:

```
proc sql;
  create table T1 as             NOTE: PROCEDURE SQL used
  select I, mod(I,4) as J              real time      16.16 seconds
  from T5E6
  where I<5e5 and calculated J   NOTE: DATA statement used
  order by I desc;                     real time       0.61 seconds
data T2;
  set T1;
  if lag(I)<50;
run;
```

This has resulted in just a slightly briefer run time, and returns do diminish as your program is more optimised, but this is not the point of this silly example. The point is that you should strive to reduce the number of steps if it makes your program faster and doesn't impact legibility in an unacceptable fashion.

Of course, each programming case will be different, and this is why this section may look crude and almost irrelevant, but it is always a good idea to keep in mind the overall program structure to decide when to reduce the number of steps or avoid redundancies.

Use a view

In some circumstances, using a view instead of an intermediate table saves time. This is especially true if the view's data is subsequently greatly summarised or reduced. When that's the case, we avoid writing out all and then reading the data generated by the view, and only write out a small fraction of it. To continue with the example above:

```proc sql;```
 ``` create view _V as```
 ``` select I, mod(I,4) as J```
 ``` from T5E6```
 ``` where I<5e5 and calculated J```
 ``` order by I desc;```
 ```data T2;```
 ``` set _V;```
 ``` if lag(I)<50;```
 ```run;```
	```NOTE: PROCEDURE SQL used```
	 ``` real time 0.02 seconds```
	
	 ```NOTE: DATA statement used```
	 ``` real time 15.58 seconds```

The view is faster here because we write out a fraction of the initial data. This is not always true however, as using a view carries an overhead, so as usual testing is best.

That's the mantra in this book if you haven't noticed: testing with your data is best.

Here is another example. Here we have monthly customer tables and monthly information tables. We want 3 years' worth of customer information using both these data sources, so we need to merge 36 customer tables and 36 information tables. Let's create the data:

```
%let nb_mths=36;
%macro create_sample;
  data %do mth=1 %to &nb_mths.;
        CUST_DATA_MTH&mth. ( keep = MTH CUSTNO VAR1-VAR50  )
        MORE_DATA_MTH&mth. ( keep = MTH CUSTNO VAR51-VAR99 )
        %end; ;
    array VAR[99] $8 ;
    do CUSTNO = 1 to 1e6;
      %do mth=1 %to &nb_mths.;
        MTH=&mth.;
        output CUST_DATA_MTH&mth. MORE_DATA_MTH&mth. ;
      %end;
    end;
  run;
%mend;
%create_sample;
```

Now we can merge these tables in a normal data step, or we can create views so that we merge data that is organised sequentially for a faster merge.

```%* Normal data step merge;```
 ```data MERGE1;```
 ```   merge CUST_DATA_MTH1-CUST_DATA_MTH&nb_mths.```
 ```   (keep=MTH CUSTNO VAR11 VAR25 VAR50)```
 ```   MORE_DATA_MTH1-MORE_DATA_MTH&nb_mths.```
 ```   (keep=MTH CUSTNO VAR61 VAR75 VAR99);```
 ```   by MTH CUSTNO;```
 ```run;```
	``` ```
	 ```NOTE: DATA statement used```
	 ``` real time 2:34:02```
	 ``` user cpu time 2:12.07```

Here, the data step opens all the tables at once and scans each of them at each iteration.

Now if we use two views:

```%* Data step merge with sequential views;```
 ```data _V_CUST/view=_V_CUST;```
 ``` set CUST_DATA_MTH1-CUST_DATA_MTH&nb_mths.```
 ```   (keep=MTH CUSTNO VAR11 VAR25 VAR50);```
 ```run;```
 ```data _V_MORE/view=_V_MORE;```
 ``` set MORE_DATA_MTH1-MORE_DATA_MTH&nb_mths.```
 ```   (keep=MTH CUSTNO VAR61 VAR75 VAR99);```
 ```run;```
 ```data MERGE2;```
 ``` merge _V_CUST```
 ```   _V_MORE;```
 ``` by MTH CUSTNO;```
 ```run;```
	``` ```
	 ```NOTE: DATA statement used```
	 ``` real time 31.98```
	 ``` user cpu time 10.81```

Here, the views enable a simple 2-way merge and only two tables are open at any point in time. Using the views speeds up the process by a factor of five.

There are many examples where using views is better than processing all the raw data as is. Experiment!

☞ Unfortunately, views are not available (yet?) to point to SPDE tables. That's a real shame as despite its many youthful flaws, SPDE's efficiency makes it the storage of choice for large data sets.

Use PROC DATASETS to modify metadata

There is no need to use a DATA step just to alter most variable or data set attributes. A DATA step will process all the data while PROC DATASETS only processes the header portion of a SAS data set.

If you are only going to alter an existing data set's metadata for information like:

- Variable format or informat,
- Variable name,
- Variable label,
- Data set name,
- Data set label,
- Passwords,

you should use PROC DATASETS to do it instantly.

For example this PROC DATASETS step:

```
proc datasets noprint;
   change SALES=SALES_SUM;
   modify SALES_SUM (label='Sales Summary' alter='mypass');
   rename SALES=SALES_TOTAL;
   attrib SALES_TOTAL format=comma12.2 label='Total Sales';
quit;
```

will do the same metadata updates as this DATA step:

```
data SALES_SUM(label='Sales Summary' alter='mypass');
   set SALES;
   attrib SALES format=comma12.2 label='Total Sales';
   rename SALES=SALES_TOTAL;
run;
```

without copying the data.

☞ Because the data isn't touched, indexes can also be added or deleted with PROC DATASETS faster than by using a DATA step, although the creation time of the index itself will remain unchanged.

☞ Only when modifying the data portion of a data set - for example to change variable length or data set compression - is a DATA step required.

Query the metadata

Whenever possible it is best to access a data set's metadata to obtain information rather than to process the data.

The SAS dictionary is a great repository of metadata. It can be slow however when multiple libraries are defined, and I usually prefer simply calling PROC CONTENTS.

PROC CONTENTS's output is quite rich and even contains centiles information for indexed variables.

The main reason I mention metadata here is that the most common metadata sought is the number of rows. Three attributes are available to describe the number of rows in a table:

- NOBS returns the number of physical rows, including delete ones.
- NLOBS returns the number of logical rows, i.e. it excludes deleted rows.
- NLOBSF returns the number of actual rows if a where clause a provided.

The first two attributes are derived from the metadata while third one requires reading the table.

Note that when using count(*), PROC SQL queries the metadata for an instant response when no WHERE clause is present, but that it scans the table if a condition is specified.

PROC SQL is much faster than attribute NLOBSF when a where clause is applied.

```
data MAIN;
  do ID=1 to 1e7;
    output;
  end;
run;

data _null_;
  DSID=open ('MAIN');
  NOBS=attrn(DSID,'NOBS');
  RC =close(DSID); run;                  real time        0.01 seconds

data _null_;
  DSID=open ('MAIN');
  NOBS=attrn(DSID,'NLOBS');
  RC =close(DSID); run;                  real time        0.01 seconds

data _null_;
  DSID=open ('MAIN');
  NOBS=attrn(DSID,'NLOBSF');
  RC =close(DSID); run;                  real time        0.01 seconds

data _null_;
  DSID=open ('MAIN(where=(ID)');
  NOBS=attrn(DSID,'NLOBSF');
  RC =close(DSID); run;                  real time       10.03 seconds

proc sql; select count(*) from MAIN;     real time        0.01 seconds

proc sql; select count(*) from TEST where ID;   real time   2.67 seconds
```

Conclusion

If you are a seasoned SAS programmer, you may think all the above points are obvious. If not, please consider each of them carefully. Endeavour to make it a habit to take into account these tips.

Here is a short story to conclude: in one of my missions, I reduced a job's run time from 2 hours to 5 minutes. I implemented some of the tips you'll find in this book, and one of the main gains was to reduce the number of data passes from a hundred to ... one. The job had to process around 50 1GB+ text files. It was reading one file in a DATA step, creating a SAS data set, appending, and starting over. I made numerous changes to the process, but one of the main gains was simply to create the final data set using only one DATA step to read all the files by making use of the FILENAME statement's FILEVAR option. Nothing extraordinary from a SAS viewpoint, but extraordinary gains.

The moral of the story is: think before you code, and try to write optimised code. Not just code that works.

Chapter 4

Sorting

Introduction

Sorting data sets is a both a common task and a resource-intensive one. This gives us a strong incentive to look at ways to optimise it and make the best use of available resources to boost its speed.

PROC SORT

We'll first have a comprehensive look at how PROC SORT works. Once we understand this, we'll be able to review the different PROC SORT options and make sense of them.

How PROC SORT works

PROC SORT performs three overlapping operations: it reads the input data, it creates its own intermediate data store, and finally it outputs the sorted data.

The first two operations (reading and sorting) take place simultaneously: the data is sorted as it is read in. The third operation is then performed separately: sorted data is written out.

If there is enough computer memory (RAM) available to fit the data, SAS performs all the sorting in memory. This is called an 'internal sort' and works extremely quickly. The alternative 'external sort' is slower and makes use of SAS 'utility files' on a hard drive. These files are used to expand the amount of space available beyond computer memory. Using the hard disk allows PROC SORT to process any amount of data, only limited by the available disk space.

Figure 4.1: Diagram of the data movements during an internal sort

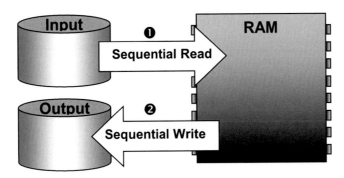

❶ Data is read and sorted in memory.
❷ The sorted data is written out.

Figure 4.2: Diagram of the data movements during an external sort

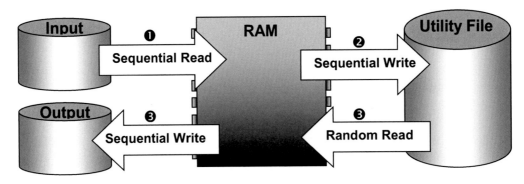

❶ Data is read and sorted in memory.
❷ Sorted data is written out to utility file(s).
Steps ❶ and ❷ are repeated until all the data is sorted.
❸ The final utility file is read and the sorted data is written out.
Note that switching from an internal sort to an external sort will dramatically slow down the sort process since it requires accessing a hard disk. This can be seen in the examples below by looking at the run times.

Example

Here we sort 1 million, then 1.2 million, then 1.5 million observations. The last sort exceeds the available memory space and must be done as an external sort (on the hard disk).

We'll use this code:

```
data SSD.T5E6(compress=no);
  length X $1016; X='1';
  do I =1 to 5e6;
    output;
  end;
run;
proc sort data=SSD.T5E6(obs=&nobs) out=T(compress=yes) sortsize=max;
  by descending I;
run;
```

Here are the logs:

```
NOTE: There were 1000000 observations read from the data set SSD.T5E6.
NOTE: The data set WORK.T has 1000000 observations and 2 variables.
...
NOTE: PROCEDURE SORT used (Total process time):
      real time            38.03 seconds
      user cpu time        5.87 seconds
      system cpu time      3.48 seconds
      memory               1053104.02k
      OS Memory            1059304.00k
```

This is our reference run: one million rows, 38 seconds.

```
NOTE: There were 1200000 observations read from the data set SSD.T5E6.
...
      real time            43.56 seconds
...
      OS Memory            1252752.00k
```

For the second run, we add 20% more data and run time increases by 13%, which seems fair.

```
NOTE: There were 1500000 observations read from the data set SSD.T5E6.
...
      real time            1:30.95
...
      OS Memory            1395888.00k
```

Finally, when we add 25% more records, the run time doubles. We've switched from an internal sort to an external sort. Using disk storage has devastated the performance of our PROC SORT.

Let's look at what happened during these three runs by looking at Windows' Task Manager.

Figure 4.3: Resources used by the three sorts in Windows' Task Manager

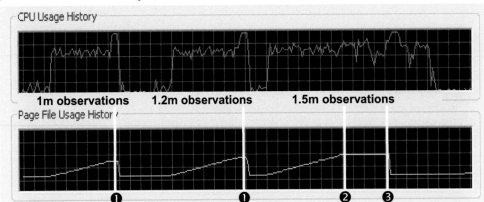

❶ This line marks the point when our first two operations have completed and all the data has been read and sorted. The write operation can start right away. Note that in our case, writing is very brief and CPU-bound; this can be seen because the CPU usage is 100%.

❷ This line marks the point when so much data has been read (and sorted as it was loaded in memory) that all the available memory has been used up. After this, more data must be loaded and SAS starts using a utility file to store the excess data.

❸ All the data has been read and sorted. At that point, SAS frees the memory and starts merging the utility file data and writing out the output file. All the data is read from disk (reading the utility file) and written to disk (writing the output file) from this point. Consequently, memory is no longer needed and is released.

If we use Windows' Performance Monitor to look at these operations in more detail, we can also watch when SAS reads and writes data.

Figure 4.4: Resources used by a 1-million-observation internal sort in Windows' Performance Monitor

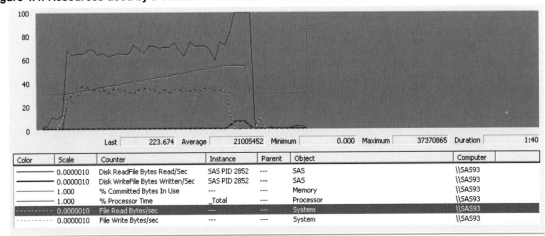

Here we again see the data being taken in and sorted, then the output file being written.

Because the output data compresses well, the output file shown by the blue (dark line at the bottom in B&W) bump is much smaller than the yellow/green (light dashes in B&W) input file.

The write speed is much lower than the read speed because it is limited by the CPU. CPU usage is 100%, and the write speed could be increased if the CPU could compress faster the data coming at high speed directly from memory.

Figure 4.5: Resources used by a 1.5-million-obs. external sort in Windows' Performance Monitor

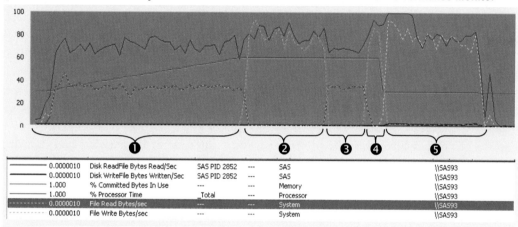

Note that SAS's WriteFile counter only monitors data written to disk via the WriteFile() API, which the utility files don't use.

Now that we have more detail, we can see clearly the five actual phases in an external PROC SORT:

❶ SAS loads the first batch of data into memory up to the maximum available, as set by either SORTSIZE or REALMEMSIZE.

❷ Since there is more data to sort, SAS writes the first run of sorted data to a utility file.

❸ SAS reads and sorts more data.

❹ SAS writes the second run to the utility file.

❺ SAS frees the allocated memory. It reads the utility file non-sequentially as it merges (technically, interleaves) the runs, and writes the sorted data to the final output file. Note that in this case, the CPU is not used to full capacity since data arrives slower for compression: Reading the utility file is the bottleneck.

Now that we understand how hardware resources are used by PROC SORT, we can look at how the PROC SORT options affect its operation.

SORTSIZE Option

SET AS: SYSTEM OPTION, PROCEDURE OPTION

This option sets the maximum amount of system memory (RAM) that the SORT procedure is able to use.

While too little memory adversely affects sorting and SAS performance, having excessively large amounts of memory available can be of no benefit. The key to determining whether additional memory might improve performance is whether or not the sort fits in memory.

If the sorted file requires more memory than is allocated, then a SORTSIZE value around 128MB is considered by some to be the optimal value. The memory can then be used for other purposes like caching, or by other applications. On the other hand, less SORTSIZE memory means that the utility file will be created in smaller sections using more runs. This in turn means more random accesses when merging, although no significant gains have been observed when increasing SORTSIZE from 64MB to 512MB. As usual, it is best to test with your data and your hardware.

☞ SORTSIZE should always be set to a value that is at least 8MB smaller than MEMSIZE. Usually, the difference will be greater than 8 MB.

☞ The default SORTSIZE value depends on the operating system.

☞ The value should not be greater than the amount of available memory. If SAS were to perform an internal sort while the OS is paging its memory calls, the performance would be much worse than doing an external sort. PROC SORT uses its utility files efficiently, writing only once, and writing sequentially.

☞ Because SAS doesn't necessarily access memory sequentially when doing internal sorts, there may be cases when performing an external sort is faster than performing an internal sort provided the utility file is located on a RAM disk.

In this case, the somewhat structured organisation of utility files can speed up memory access. In technical terms, the external sort's memory access pattern may be better due to increased spatial locality of reference (i.e. when a location is referenced, it is very probable that locations that are physically close to it will be referenced as well), and memory optimisation techniques like caching can take advantage of this. This is not step one of sort optimisation, but it's worth keeping in mind if you run out of options to save time and can free up memory for RAM disks.

☞ Precedence: If the SORTSIZE option is not used in a PROC SORT statement, PROC SORT uses the value of the SORTSIZE system option; otherwise as expected the SORTSIZE option specified in PROC SORT overrides the system option.

PRESORTED Option

SET AS: PROCEDURE OPTION, SYSTEM OPTION (SORTVALIDATE)

SAS data sets contain rich metadata. Two interesting pieces of metadata about data ordering are the SORTED flag and its partner, the VALIDATED flag. These flags can be set to Yes or No and are visible in the output of the CONTENTS procedure.

SORTED=Y indicates that the data set is sorted. This flag can be set automatically by SAS or manually.

If the SORTED flag equals Y, then the VALIDATED flag is set to Y automatically, to indicate that SAS has validated that the data set is indeed sorted. This information is used to optimise data processing; it's a desirable piece of metadata to have attached to a file.

If the VALIDATED flag is set to No, it's probably because the data set has been created using the SORTEDBY= data set option. Here are examples.

```
data OUT;  ...  run;
```
The data set defined above contains the metadata SORTED=N.

```
data OUT(sortedby=I);  ...  run;
```
This data set contains the metadata SORTED=Y, VALIDATED=N.

```
proc sort out=OUT;  ...  run;
```
This data set contains the metadata SORTED=Y, VALIDATED=Y.

Wouldn't it be nice for us to have a data set option that checks the sort order as the data set is written out? Something like the imaginary option below:

```
data OUT(sortedby=I sortvalidate); … ;run; /* INVALID SYNTAX */
```

This would avoid having to sort just to set the VALIDATED flag.

✋ Please SAS Institute: You know you want to create this option. And while you're at it, can you please save the VALIDATED flag when a table is uploaded so we don't have to run PROC SORT then just to restore the flag?

Such a data set option is not available yet, however there are still ways to avoid sorting. We can ask SAS to simply validate the sort order and do a straight copy of a data set. This is what PROC SORT's PRESORTED option does.

When option PRESORTED is used, the SORT procedure performs a sequence check to ensure that the data set is sorted according to the BY statement. If the data set isn't sorted correctly, SAS sorts the data set normally. If it is sorted correctly, PROC SORT copies the data. Either way SAS will set both SORTED and VALIDATED flags to Y, as it knows these are both true.

Why does the VALIDATED flag matter?

There is very little documentation around this matter: various procedures will use data set metadata in different ways. By way of an example, let's look at the SQL procedure.

Example 1 - SORTED=N

```
data OUT;
  do I=1 to 5e6;
    output;
  end;
run;
proc sql _method noprint;
  create table A as
  select T1.I
  from OUT T1
     , OUT T2
  where T1.I=T2.I;
quit;
```

Not knowing any better, the SQL procedure optimizer performs a hash join operation (SQJHSH) which takes a long time:

```
 proc sql _method noprint;
    create table A as
    select T1.I
    from T T1
       , T T2
    where T1.I=T2.I;
NOTE: SQL execution methods chosen are:
      sqxcrta
         sqxjhsh
             sqxsrc( WORK.OUT(alias = T1) )
             sqxsrc( WORK.OUT(alias = T2) )
NOTE: Table WORK.A created, with 5000000 rows and 1 columns.
   quit;
NOTE: PROCEDURE SQL used (Total process time):
      real time            15.79 seconds
      cpu time             8.88 seconds
```

Example 2 - SORTED=Y, VALIDATED=N

```
data OUT(sortedby=I);
  do I=1 to 5e6;
    output;
  end;
run;
proc sql _method noprint;
  create table A as
  select T1.I
  from OUT T1
     , OUT T2
  where T1.I=T2.I;
quit;
```

The SQL procedure optimiser has more information this time and decides to perform a sort join operation (SQXJM) which takes less time:

```
  proc sql _method noprint;
    create table A as
    select T1.I
    from OUT T1
       , OUT T2
    where T1.I=T2.I;
NOTE: SQL execution methods chosen are:
      sqxcrta
        sqxjm
            sqxsrc( WORK.OUT(alias = T1) )
            sqxsrc( WORK.OUT(alias = T2) )
NOTE: Table WORK.A created, with 5000000 rows and 1 columns.
  quit;
NOTE: PROCEDURE SQL used (Total process time):
      real time           7.67 seconds
      cpu time            3.97 seconds
```

Example 3 - SORTED=Y, VALIDATED=Y

```
data OUT;
  do I=1 to 5e6;
    output;
  end;
run;

proc sort presorted; by I; run;

proc sql _method noprint;
  create table A as
  select T1.I
  from OUT T1
     , OUT T2
  where T1.I=T2.I;
quit;
```

The SQL procedure still performs a sort join operation, but uses the VALIDATED flag and runs consistently faster, probably because it foregoes data order validation. This saves about 1 second of real time and half a second of CPU time: a 10% and 15% reduction respectively:

```
  proc sort presorted; by I; run;

NOTE: Sort order of input data set has been verified.
NOTE: There were 5000000 observations read from the data set WORK.OUT.
NOTE: Input data set is already sorted, no sorting done.
NOTE: PROCEDURE SORT used (Total process time):
      real time           3.35 seconds
      cpu time            0.80 seconds

  proc sql _method noprint;
    create table A as
    select T1.I
```

```
    from OUT T1
       , OUT T2
    where T1.I=T2.I;
NOTE: SQL execution methods chosen are:
      sqxcrta
          sqxjm
              sqxsrc( WORK.OUT(alias = T1) )
              sqxsrc( WORK.OUT(alias = T2) )
NOTE: Table WORK.A created, with 5000000 rows and 1 columns.
  quit;
NOTE: PROCEDURE SQL used (Total process time):
      real time           6.87 seconds
      cpu time            3.38 seconds
```

Did you notice the following line at the top of the log? PROC SORT had an easy job and ran faster.

```
NOTE: Sort order of input data set has been verified.
```

In the above example, for one-off use, there is no benefit in running PROC SORT just to set the VALIDATED flag. If however the table will be queried repeatedly (for example if it's part of a data mart), it is well worth setting the VALIDATED flag. Doing so will ensure SAS uses the various performance enhancements that take advantage of a verified sort order.

☞ By default, PROC SORT will always sort unless SORTED equals Y.

☞ Conversely, PROC SORT will never sort if SORTED equals Y.
If SORTED equals Y (even if VALIDATED=N), the following note will be written in the log:

```
NOTE: Input data set is already sorted, no sorting done.
```
🏳 **Danger: This note appears and the data is left as is, even if the data is not sorted.**

☞ The PRESORTED option changes the default behaviour and skips sorting even if SORTED=N, provided the sequence verification is successful and the data is indeed found to be sorted.

☞ Even if the SORTED flag equals Y, PROC SORT can be forced to sort the data by using the FORCE option.

☞ The PROC SORT option PRESORTED can be replaced by the system option SORTVALIDATE. When SORTVALIDATE is set, PROC SORT performs a sequence check whenever it encounters a data set whose metadata contains SORTED=Y and VALIDATED=N.

For example:

```
data OUT(sortedby=I);
...
option sortvalidate;
proc sort; by I; run;
```

is equivalent to

```
data OUT(sortedby=I);
...;
proc sort presorted; by I; run;
```

⚑ **A small warning**: When the PROC SORT option NODUPKEY is used with option PRESORTED (or the SORTVALIDATE option), PROC SORT will assume that the data has unique keys. If it has duplicate keys, PROC SORT will consider it has been given incorrect information and it will sort the data again. It will also write this protestation in the log:

```
NOTE: Input data set is not in sorted order.
NOTE: SAS sort was used.
```

TAGSORT Option

SET AS: PROCEDURE OPTION

TAGSORT is not an option originally intended to increase performance. On the contrary, this option may significantly slow down some sorting processes. Why use it then? We may wish to use since it allows us to sort large SAS data sets, even when we don't have enough disk space for a regular sort process.

How does this work? From the SAS documentation:

"When you specify the TAGSORT option, only sort keys (that is, the variables specified in the BY statement) and the observation number for each observation are stored in the temporary files, so much less data is sorted. The sort keys, together with the observation number, are referred to as tags. At the completion of the sorting process, the tags are used to retrieve the records from the input data set in sorted order. Thus, in cases where the total number of bytes of the sort keys is small compared with the length of the record, temporary disk use is reduced considerably. However, you should have enough disk space to hold another copy of the data (the output data set) or two copies of the tags, whichever is greater. Note that although using the TAGSORT option can reduce temporary disk use, the processing time might be much higher."

The processing time can be (much) higher for two reasons:

- After sorting, the data must be read again from the source table. Not sequentially. This not good. This is apparent in the log, where a note informs us:

```
NOTE: Tagsort reads each observation of the input data set twice.
```

- The TAGSORT option is not supported in multi-threaded sorts, so the sort will be single-threaded. This may not matter too much though: if the data set to sort is so large that TAGSORT must be used, it's likely that the operation will be time-bound by hard disk speed, not CPU speed.

The processing time can be lower in some cases however, and that's where it becomes interesting for us. We can save time when the tag size is a small fraction of the observation length and the data set is already somewhat sorted. Since TAGSORT sorts a small amount of data (the tag) we will save resources overall.

Let's look:

Example 1 – Normal sort

```
data SSD.T5E6;
  length X $1016; X='1';
  do I=1 to 5e6;
    output;
  end;
run;
proc sort data=SSD.T5E6 out=T(compress=yes) sortsize=max;
  by I;
run;
```

```
real time         5:18.49
user cpu time     21.67 seconds
system cpu time   27.75 seconds
memory            1,508,109k
OS Memory         1,514,792k
```

The sort runs in 5min 18s, using significant memory resource and paging along the way.

Example 2 – Tag sort, data in order with respect to the BY variable

```
proc sort data=SSD.T5E6 out=T(compress=yes) sortsize=max tagsort;
  by I;
run
```

```
real time         3:43.57
user cpu time     19.05 seconds
system cpu time   9.88 seconds
memory            139,682k
OS Memory         146,276k
```

Here we use much less memory and the run time has shrunk by 25%.

Because the tag was much smaller than the full record, and because the source data didn't have to be accessed in a totally random manner after the sort, this is actually more efficient as we didn't have to create huge utility files. In this case the sort became internal. Elapse time, CPU and memory usage are all noticeably lower as well.

Example 3 – Tag sort, data is extremely out of order with respect to the BY variable

```
proc sort data=SSD.T5E6 out=T(compress=yes) sortsize=max tagsort;
  by descending I;
run
```

real time	5:54.68
user cpu time	16.79 seconds
system cpu time	9.58 seconds
memory	139,681k
OS Memory	146,276k

This time the performance is worse, but not by much.

The time saved by the very small sort partially counterbalances the time wasted to randomly fetch the input data after the sort. This will be true only when the ratio sort-key-length to record-length is very small. While elapse time is higher, the resource footprint is smaller than for the full sort.

The TAGSORT option is usually best avoided, but there are instances where it proves indispensable to complete sorts on large tables, or even useful to boost speed when it prevents paging. So keep this option in mind, but use it appropriately.

Faster than PROC SORT?

This section moves beyond options, but since we started experimenting with alternative ways to sort, we may as well continue our journey a bit further.

In particular, we can manage our sort manually, or use PROC SQL, or use no procedure at all, and compare with the measures made in the first example.

Example 4 – Can we beat SAS by managing the sort manually?
In this example, we know that we have data that compresses really well and we use this characteristic to our advantage. We can replicate SAS's external sort logic by running multiple internal sorts, and while doing so we'll compress the intermediate utility files. SAS doesn't compress utility files.

The small macro below does this for us.

```
%macro split_sort(dsin=, split_obs=, compress=yes,by=, dsout=_SORTED);

  * Initialise;
  %local run runs;
  data _null_;
    set &dsin. nobs=NOBS;
    call symputx('runs',ceil(NOBS/&split_obs.));
    stop;
  run;
```

```
 * Sort;
%do run=1 %to &runs.;
    proc sort data    = &dsin.(firstobs= %eval((&run.-1)*&split_obs.+1)
                               obs      = %eval(&run.*&split_obs.) )
                out    = _TMP_SORT&run.(compress=&compress)
                sortsize= max;
      by &by.;
    run;
%end;

 * Merge;
data &dsout.(compress=&compress);
    set _TMP_SORT1 - _TMP_SORT&runs.;
    by &by.;
run;

 * Clean up;
proc datasets noprint;
    delete _TMP_SORT:;
  quit;
%mend;

%split_sort(dsin=SSD.T5E6, split_obs=1000000, by=descending I );
```

```
NOTE: PROCEDURE SORT used (Total process time):
      real time           31.69 seconds
...
      real time           36.20 seconds
...
      real time           37.93 seconds
...
      real time           37.20 seconds
...
      real time           35.79 seconds
...
NOTE: There were 1000000 observations read from the data set WORK._TMP_SORT1.
...
NOTE: There were 1000000 observations read from the data set WORK._TMP_SORT5.
NOTE: The data set WORK._SORTED has 5000000 observations and 2 variables.
NOTE: Compressing data set WORK._SORTED decreased size by 98.04 percent.
      Compressed is 6531 pages; un-compressed would require 333334 pages.
NOTE: DATA statement used (Total process time):
      real time           22.37 seconds
```

The total time is five lots of 36 seconds plus 22s: a grand total of 202 seconds.

This is 2/3 of the normal sort time in our first example, and the fastest sort of all our attempts.

This shows the potential power of manually managing such sorts. Of course, most real-world data will not compress as well as our sample data, but there are cases where it will compress well enough to consider manually bypassing SAS's uncompressed utility files.

✋ Please SAS Institute: Can you please make sorts faster by compressing data in the utility files to reduce IOs, and in memory to avoid externals sorts?

Example 5 – How about sorting with PROC SQL?
Have you ever wondered whether PROC SQL is as fast as PROC SORT for sorting?

Well in either case, as we are in this together, you officially have now. Let's see... we'll start with running an external sort.

```
option sortsize=1g;
proc sql;
  create table _SORTED(compress=yes) as
  select *
  from SSD.T5E6
  order by I desc;
quit;
```

PROC SQL is limited by the SORTSIZE system option, so after making sure this option is set appropriately, we can verify below that PROC SQL has the same sorting speed as PROC SORT. This is still an important result: PROC SQL has interesting features for sorted data. We'll look at them later.

```
NOTE: PROCEDURE SQL used (Total process time):
      real time           5:23.55
      user cpu time       41.60 seconds
      system cpu time     40.19 seconds
      memory              1050230.11k
      OS Memory           1063800.00k
```

We can do the same verification with an internal sort:

```
proc sql;
  create table _SORTED(compress=yes) as
  select *
  from SSD.T5E6(obs=1000000)
  order by I desc;
quit;
```

```
      real time           39.04 seconds
      user cpu time       5.84 seconds
      system cpu time     4.11 seconds
      memory              1023380.21k
      OS Memory           1030248.00k
```

Example 6 – How about sorting with a hash table?

The hash table can use a logic similar to that of the internal sort, and by default it de-duplicates keys. But how fast is it? Let's compare to the one million-row internal sort above.

```
data _null_;
  if 0 then set SSD.T5E6;
  dcl hash H(dataset:'SSD.T5E6(obs=1000000)', ordered:'a');
  H.definekey('I');
  H.definedata(ALL:'yes');
  H.definedone();
  H.output(dataset:'_S(compress=y)');
run;
```

The hash table takes longer, and is more resource intensive.

real time	41.94 seconds
user cpu time	11.82 seconds
system cpu time	2.50 seconds
memory	1086207.82k
OS Memory	1095744.00k

The difference in performance is not catastrophic though. Using hash tables may still be useful if you need both to sort data and to process it in a DATA step: the sorted table is read and loaded in memory once, ready to be processed in the DATA step, and you don't need to run PROC SORT.

Example 7 - Not enough memory or disk space? Indexes can help

If the sort process uses too much memory, avoiding PROC SORT and instead using an index to construct the sorted data set may be a prudent (if not always faster) option.

```
proc sql;
  create index I on SSD.T5E6;
quit;
data T(compress=yes);
  set SSD.T5E6;
  by I;
run;
```

This takes a bit more time than using PROC SORT, but requires much less memory and disk space.

```
NOTE: Simple index I has been defined.
...
NOTE: PROCEDURE SQL used (Total process time):
      real time          2:58.39
      user cpu time      11.94 seconds
      system cpu time    16.05 seconds
      memory             201960.71k
      OS Memory          216456.00k
...
INFO: Index I selected for BY clause processing.
...
NOTE: DATA statement used (Total process time):
      real time          3:21.65
      user cpu time      35.55 seconds
      system cpu time    12.67 seconds
      memory             369.85k
      OS Memory          14960.00k
```

As for the hash table example, if the sorted data set is to subsequently be processed by a DATA step, this method may actually be faster than using PROC SORT. This is because we go directly from the unsorted table to the processed table, bypassing the creation of an intermediate sorted table.

☞ Like example 6, this method will not set the VALIDATED flag. Use PROC SORT with its PRESORTED option after the code above if you need to set this flag; it uses fewer resources compared to an actual sort as it only copies the data.

NOEQUALS

SET AS: PROCEDURE OPTION, SYSTEM OPTION (NOSORTEQUALS)

By default, the EQUALS option is set and PROC SORT keeps observations with identical BY-variable values in the same order in the output data set as they are in the input data set. This often adds no value to the process.

For multi-threaded sorts, the NOEQUALS option stops SAS's efforts to preserve this order in the output data set. When using this option, the order of observations within BY groups which have identical BY values might not be consistent between runs.

☞ Using procedure option NOEQUALS can save CPU time and memory.

☞ The NOEQUALS and NOEQUALS options have no effect on single-threaded sorts.

☞ It may be useful to set the system option NOSORTEQUALS as a default in order to improve the performance of all sorts.

NODUP

SET AS: PROCEDURE OPTION

A brief exception to this book being all about performance: This page isn't, rather it is about dispelling a very common misconception: the idea that the PROC SORT option NODUP or NODUPRECS simply removes duplicate observations.

Here is an exercise. How many observations do you think table T1 will contain?

```
data T;
  X=1; Z=3; output;
  X=1; Z=4; output;
  X=1; Z=3; output;
 proc sort data=T out=T1 nodup;
  by X;
run;
```

Don't look below yet, come up with an answer first.

Observations 1 and 3 are the same, correct? Hence we should drop one observation... correct?

Here is what the SAS documentation states: Option NODUPRECS *"checks for and eliminates duplicate observations. If you specify this option, then PROC SORT compares all variable values for each observation to the ones for the previous observation that was written to the output data set. If an exact match is found, then the observation is not written to the output data set."*

So 2 observations in data set T1? Read again.

Here is the log generated:

```
NOTE: There were 3 observations read from the data set WORK.T.
NOTE: 0 duplicate observations were deleted.
NOTE: The data set WORK.T1 has 3 observations and 3 variables.
```

The documentation also states: *"Because NODUPRECS checks only consecutive observations, some non-consecutive duplicate observations might remain in the output data set. You can remove all duplicates with this option by sorting on all variables."* So to achieve a no duplicate observations, it is best to sort BY _ALL_, or at least to sort on variables that create a unique identifier.

Now you know (if you didn't already).

🖑 **Option NODUP will not always delete duplicate records**

UBUFSIZE & UBUFNO

SET AS: SYSTEM OPTION AT STARTUP

Like BUFSIZE and BUFNO, these options set the size of data buffers when accessing files. They are specific to utility files and may benefit from being given a boost from their default values. As usual, results can vary and testing for the best values in each case may be worthwhile.

Disk Space: OVERWRITE

SET AS: PROCEDURE OPTION

PROC SORT can be rather disk space-hungry. SAS Institute advises that we need a free amount of disk space equal to three to four times the uncompressed input data set size. So if we are sorting 1 GB, we should have 3 to 4 GB free. If the output data set is compressed, we may need less.

Maybe one day there will exist an option to compress utility files. In the meantime, and if you really can't use internal sorts (in small subsets of the input data set), there is a way to lower disk space requirements provided you replace the input data with the sorted data on the fly. This is done with PROC SORT option OVERWRITE. When this option is used, the source data set is deleted just prior to the output data set being created.

There are a few caveats however:

- The input data set is deleted as soon as the final output phase starts, so if this phase fails, the input data is lost.
- The output data set must be the same as the input data set, so the OVERWRITE option has no effect when an OUT= data set is specified.
- The OVERWRITE option is supported by SAS sort and SAS multi-threaded sort only. The option has no effect if you are using a host sort such as Syncsort.
- The OVERWRITE option has no effect if you also specify the TAGSORT option since TAGSORT must read the input data set while populating the output data set.

If these constraints are acceptable, the OVERWRITE option is a good way to reduce PROC SORT's disk space requirements.

Only use this option if you are prepared to lose your data in case of a problem during the sort.

The best sort never takes place

Remove unnecessary sorts

This last section is the most obvious one. It is not uncommon as one follows an algorithm's logic to sort several times in order to get the data in the desired shape. Just by keeping an awareness of when a sort is needed and when one is not needed, we can reap very large dividends. Consider the following simple example:

Example 1- Simple code

```
proc sort data=SASHELP.CLASS out=T;
  by AGE;
proc summary data=T noprint nway;
  by AGE;
  output out=AGES;
proc sort data=SASHELP.CLASS out=T;
  by SEX;
proc freq data=T;
  tables SEX;
proc sort data=SASHELP.CLASS out=T;
  by AGE NAME;
proc print data=T;
 by AGE NAME;
run;
```

Example 2 - Two out of three sorts are unnecessary

Example 1 can easily be re-written as:

```
proc summary data=SASHELP.CLASS noprint nway;
  class AGE;
  output out=AGES;
proc freq data=SASHELP.CLASS;
  tables SEX;
proc sort data=SASHELP.CLASS out=T;
  by AGE NAME;
proc print data=T;
  by AGE NAME;
run;
```

Example 3 - Optimise further

Since there will be a sort anyway, we can sort first and optimise PROC SUMMARY by replacing the CLASS statement with a BY statement:

```
proc sort data=SASHELP.CLASS out=T;
  by AGE NAME;
proc summary data=T noprint;
  by AGE;
  output out=AGES;
proc freq data=T;
  tables SEX;
proc print data=T;
  by AGE NAME;
run;
```

The BY statement makes PROC SUMMARY summarise each BY group as an independent subset of the input data. This significantly reduces memory requirements but can (surprisingly) increase run time.

✍ Please SAS Institute: Make BY groups more efficient than CLASS groups.

Use an index

We can avoid sorting altogether by using an index.

Again, it can be worth checking if creating and using an index will work better in your specific case.

Example 4 - Index
The example below is the same as Example 3 except that we create an index rather than sorting.

```
proc sql;
   create index AGENAME on SASHELP.CLASS (AGE, NAME);
proc summary data= SASHELP.CLASS noprint;
   by AGE;
   output out=AGES;
proc freq data= SASHELP.CLASS;
   tables SEX;
proc print data=SASHELP.CLASS;
   by AGE NAME;
run;
```

On-the-fly implicit sorting

One of the features of the SDPE engine is its ability to sort data on the fly as needed, and this works quite well. See the section in chapter 6 about on-the-fly implicit sorting.

NOTSORTED

The NOTSORTED option allows us to process data that is grouped, but where the groups are in no particular order.

Say you regularly append surveys to a survey table. The survey IDs in the data set will be ordered randomly, but you know that all observations for a given survey are grouped together.

Here we can avoid sorting.

The syntax applicable to such a 'grouped-but-not-sorted' data set looks like this:

```
data ANALYSIS;
  set SURVEYS;
  by SURVEY notsorted;
  ... more code
run;
```

When we avoid sorting, our performance gain is 100%. So we should always consider what our program does and its overall organisation. This may be where the biggest performance improvements lie.

Unfortunately for some (although no one is reading this of course), our own minds are where the biggest performance improvements typically lie.

DETAILS

The DETAILS option displays many of PROC SORT's internal parameters. In practice, this option will mostly be used by programmers to determine the type of sort that takes place.

As an exercise, we sort a table and gradually reduce the amount of memory available to PROC SORT in order to degrade its performance. As PROC SORT goes through different algorithms to accommodate its execution environment, it gives information about its execution choices.

Here is the code:

```
option fullstimer msglevel=I cpucount=2 compress=no;

data TMP; do I=1 to 1e6; output; end; run;

*Test1; proc sort data=TMP out=TMP1 sortsize=90000k details; by I; run;
*Test2; proc sort data=TMP out=TMP1 sortsize= 9000k details; by I; run;
*Test3; proc sort data=TMP out=TMP1 sortsize= 2300k details; by I; run;
*Test4; proc sort data=TMP out=TMP1 sortsize=  900k details; by I; run;
*Test5; proc sort data=TMP out=TMP1 sortsize=   90k details; by I; run;
*Test6; proc sort data=TMP(obs=99)  sortsize=90000k details; by I; run;
```

Here is the log:

```
500   *Test1;
500!          proc sort data=TMP out=TMP1 sortsize=90000k details; by I; run;

NOTE: Compression was disabled for data set WORK.TMP1 because compression overhead would
increase the size of the data set.
NOTE: There were 1000000 observations read from the data set WORK.TMP.
NOTE: Sort completed in memory.
NOTE: SAS threaded sort was used.
NOTE: The data set WORK.TMP1 has 1000000 observations and 1 variables.
NOTE: PROCEDURE SORT used (Total process time):
      real time            0.12 seconds
      user cpu time        0.25 seconds
      system cpu time      0.00 seconds
      Memory                          48033k
      OS Memory                       60704k
      Timestamp          5/12/2014  4:59:46 p.m.
```

```
501  *Test2;
501!        proc sort data=TMP out=TMP1 sortsize= 9000k details; by I; run;

NOTE: Compression was disabled for data set WORK.TMP1 because compression overhead would
increase the size of the data set.
NOTE: Utility file required.
NOTE: Utility file 1 page size is 65536 bytes.
NOTE: There were 1000000 observations read from the data set WORK.TMP.
NOTE: Utility file 1 contains 1000000 records and 6 sorted runs.
NOTE: Utility file 1 contains 246 pages for a total of 15744.00 KB.
NOTE: SAS threaded sort was used.
NOTE: The data set WORK.TMP1 has 1000000 observations and 1 variables.
NOTE: PROCEDURE SORT used (Total process time):
      real time           0.17 seconds
      user cpu time       0.31 seconds
      system cpu time     0.03 seconds
      Memory                         10064k
      OS Memory                      22724k
      Timestamp              5/12/2014  4:59:46 p.m.


502  *Test3;
502!        proc sort data=TMP out=TMP1 sortsize= 2300k details; by I; run;

NOTE: Compression was disabled for data set WORK.TMP1 because compression overhead would
increase the size of the data set.
NOTE: Utility file required.
NOTE: Utility file 1 page size is 65536 bytes.
NOTE: There were 1000000 observations read from the data set WORK.TMP.
NOTE: Utility file 1 contains 1000000 records and 21 sorted runs.
NOTE: Utility file 1 contains 246 pages for a total of 15744.00 KB.
NOTE: Multi-pass merge.
NOTE: Second utility file required.
NOTE: Utility file 2 page size is 65536 bytes.
NOTE: Merge pass 1: merging 21 sorted runs, 5 at a time, from utility file 1.
NOTE: Utility file 2 contains 1000000 records and 1 sorted runs.
NOTE: Utility file 2 contains 245 pages for a total of 15680.00 KB.
NOTE: Merge pass 2: merging 1 sorted runs, 1 at a time, from utility file 2.
NOTE: Merge of initial set of sorted runs required 2 passes.
NOTE: SAS threaded sort was used.
NOTE: The data set WORK.TMP1 has 1000000 observations and 1 variables.
NOTE: PROCEDURE SORT used (Total process time):
      real time           0.18 seconds
      user cpu time       0.32 seconds
      system cpu time     0.04 seconds
      Memory                         3283k
      OS Memory                      15628k
      Timestamp              5/12/2014  4:59:46 p.m.
```

```
503  *Test4;
503!            proc sort data=TMP out=TMP1 sortsize=  900k details; by I; run;

NOTE: Compression was disabled for data set WORK.TMP1 because compression overhead would
increase the size of the data set.
NOTE: There were 1000000 observations read from the data set WORK.TMP.
mrgcount = 1
mempage=16384 alocsize=5488 isa=16384 osa=16384 xmisa=0
holds=682 nway=42 sortsize=921600 memoryuse=918624.00
keylen=16 reclen=8 dkin=0 inrec=1000000 outrec=1000000 yieldobs=1000
nruns=35 xcbpage=16384 npages=1468 diskuse=24051712.00


NOTE: SAS sort was used.
NOTE: The data set WORK.TMP1 has 1000000 observations and 1 variables.
NOTE: PROCEDURE SORT used (Total process time):
      real time             0.26 seconds
      user cpu time         0.18 seconds
      system cpu time       0.07 seconds
      Memory                          1139k
      OS Memory                       13872k
      Timestamp             5/12/2014  4:59:47 p.m.


504  *Test5;
504!            proc sort data=TMP out=TMP1 sortsize=   90k details; by I; run;

NOTE: Compression was disabled for data set WORK.TMP1 because compression overhead would
increase the size of the data set.
Multiway merge. To avoid increase sortsize to 834K
NOTE: There were 1000000 observations read from the data set WORK.TMP.
mrgcount = 5
mempage=16384 alocsize=5488 isa=16384 osa=16384 xmisa=0
holds=682 nway=4 sortsize=92160 memoryuse=87488.00
keylen=16 reclen=8 dkin=0 inrec=1000000 outrec=1000000 yieldobs=1000
nruns=367 xcbpage=16384 npages=2935 diskuse=48087040.00


NOTE: SAS sort was used.
NOTE: The data set WORK.TMP1 has 1000000 observations and 1 variables.
NOTE: PROCEDURE SORT used (Total process time):
      real time             0.43 seconds
      user cpu time         0.39 seconds
      system cpu time       0.04 seconds
      Memory                          306k
      OS Memory                       13360k
      Timestamp             5/12/2014  4:59:47 p.m.
```

```
505  *Test6;
505!        proc sort data=TMP(obs=99)  sortsize=90000k details; by I; run;

NOTE: There were 99 observations read from the data set WORK.TMP.
mempage=16384 alocsize=5488 isa=16384 osa=16384 xmisa=0
holds=682 nway=1 sortsize=92160000 memoryuse=21872.00
keylen=16 reclen=8 dkin=0 inrec=99 outrec=99 yieldobs=1000
nruns=1 xcbpage=16384 npages=0 diskuse=0.00


NOTE: SAS sort was used.
NOTE: The data set WORK.TMP has 99 observations and 1 variables.
NOTE: PROCEDURE SORT used (Total process time):
      real time            0.00 seconds
      user cpu time        0.00 seconds
      system cpu time      0.00 seconds
      Memory                        141k
      OS Memory                     13360k
      Timestamp           5/12/2014  4:59:47 p.m.
```

Test 1 - This is the ideal execution: an internal sort takes place. SAS doesn't have much to say, and the only thing to look at is the amount of RAM used.

The internal sort is indicated by the note:

```
NOTE: Sort completed in memory.
```

Test 2 - A utility file is used, the note in the log then states:

```
NOTE: Utility file required.
```

This hinders performance as we've seen.

Test 3 - Here the performance worsens: one utility file wasn't enough, and mention of a subsequent utility file appears, accompanied with the notes:

```
NOTE: Multi-pass merge.
NOTE: Second utility file required.
```

There is a woefully insufficient amount of RAM for the sort at hand.

If the volume of data increases, several utility files may be required.

Test 4 - In this extreme condition, a single-threaded sort is used. The decision to switch to a single-threaded sort is made by an algorithm of proc SORT's, which switches to a single-threaded sort when there is a low number of observations, or when there is less than 2 MB of sort size memory available.

Obviously, options THREADS=NO or CPUCOUNT=1 will also trigger single-threaded sorts.

In Test4, because we are under the 2 MB threshold, single-threaded sort is used.

A single-threaded sort is indicated by the note:

```
NOTE: SAS sort was used.
```

instead of:

```
NOTE: SAS threaded sort was used.
```

and by the appearance of a list of operational parameter values. These parameters are only listed when single-thread sort is used.

Test 5 and Test 6 show more outputs from the single-thread sort. Test 5 shows that unsurprisingly, the number of runs increases when we reduce the amount of memory available. Test 6 shows that having few observations triggers the single-threaded sort.

Ancillary information

The information above is all we need to know for practical purposes, we don't need additional information about PROC SORT in order to make a program faster. If you want to better understand the material displayed in the log, here are a more details.

Q - What happens between Test3 and Test2 (2300k and 9000k) when 2 utility files are used instead of 1, and why use a second utility file when all the records fit in one?

A - When a sort cannot be completed within memory, a file is used to hold partial results called "sorted runs". Sorted runs are formed by reading a portion of the input into memory, sorting it, and writing it out to the file. The process of forming sorted runs repeats until the input is exhausted. Once all sorted runs (partial results) are written to the file then they must be combined to form the desired result of the sort. If the number of runs is large and the resources available are low, then it might not be possible to merge (or rather interleave, in data step parlance) all of the sorted runs at once to the final, single sorted output.

The number of sorted runs initially depends on the amount of data to sort, and on the amount of memory available for sorting. If the number of sorted runs is so large that not all runs can be merged together in one step, then they are merged in smaller groups to form new sorted runs in another file (or files). At that point, there will be fewer (but longer) runs in the second file and it might be possible to merge them all together at once to the final output – or it might not. If not, then the process of merging them to another file is done again (and again) until the set of runs is small enough to merge at one time to the final output. This case, when the initial set of sorted runs in the file cannot be merged directly to the output, is referred to as a multi-pass merge.

Note that the use of a single file versus multiple files (say, one file per sorted run) is an implementation detail. The SAS sorts store multiple sorted runs in a single file.

Q - What happens between 2300k and 900k, when utility files are still used, but the information in the log is different?

A - We have switched from a multi-threaded sort to a single-threaded sort, and details about the single-threaded run are output. Because we use a single-threaded run, CPU usage drops significantly.

Note the parameter `mrgcount` which indicates what type of sort was used.

If `mrgcount` is not displayed, the sort is internal, as seen in Test 6.

If `mrgcount`=1, we have a utility file that can build the final file with only one pass, as seen in test 4.

If `mrgcount`>1, we have a utility file that requires multiple passes to build the final file, as seen in test 5.

The message
```
Multiway merge. To avoid increase sortsize to xxxK
```
is then displayed, indicating a situation similar to that of test 3.

Note that the terms Multiway merge (Test 5) and Multi-pass merge (Test 3) mean the same thing. The former simply applies to single-threaded sorts, while the latter applies to multi-threaded sorts.

Q - This is not seen in this benchmark, but the value of option UBUFNO seems to have no influence. What's going on?

A - The UBUFNO option does not affect either the single-threaded or multi-threaded sort. Both sorts automatically manage the number of buffers they acquire and use.

Q - How does PROC SORT use the option UTILLOC?

A - The UTILLOC= option only affects the location of the utility files when the multi-threaded SAS sort is used. The multi-threaded sort stores all temporary data in a single utility file within one of the locations that are specified by the UTILLOC= system option. A second utility file of the same size can be created in another of these locations when the amount of data that is read from the input data set is large compared to the amount of memory available to the SORT procedure.

Q- What do all the variables displayed for single-threaded sorts mean?

A - These variables are not useful to SAS code programmers. They are used by the developers of PROC SORT. For information, here are some explanations.

Procedure parameters:

`mrgcount` : Number of times data must be read from one utility file and written to another (i.e., the number of passes in a multi-pass merge).

`nruns` : Number of sorted runs necessary to completely read the source data and build the (first) utility file.

`sortsize=` usually has the same value as the SORTSIZE option but might be lower

`reclen=` is the length of the buffer that can hold a record of the sorted data. Using the KEEP, DROP and TAGSORT keywords can shorten the record length. Option COMPRESS= cannot as utility files are not compressed.

`keylen=` is generally the sum of the lengths of the sort keys + ~8 bytes

`inrec=` is the number of observations read by the procedure. A WHERE clause can lower this figure.

`outrec=` is the number of observations written out by the procedure. The NODUPKEY and NODUPREC options can lower this figure.

`memoryuse=` is the memory used for storing the data that is being sorted.

Utility file parameters:

`mempage=` generally uses the value of the UBUFSIZE option, but is also influenced by other factors, such as the value of the STRIPESIZE option.

`npages=` is the number of pages in the utility file.

`diskuse=` is the amount of storage space used by utility files and is equivalent to: `mempage` times `npages`.

Other Sort Options

Other sort-related options can be seen by running:

```
proc options group=sort; run;
```

Conclusion

PROC SORT is a cornerstone of many SAS jobs. It is also one of the most resource-intensive procedures in the SAS quiver. This chapter should have helped you understand its inner workings and the different ways it can be tweaked to achieve the best possible outcome when sorted data is desirable.

Whenever you encounter a problem, if your PROC SORT is too slow, or runs out of memory or disk space, this chapter should hopefully help you find a solution.

90

Chapter 5

SAS Options Affecting Performance

Introduction

Various SAS options can be used to monitor resource consumption or optimize job performance. Some of these options can have a dramatic impact on the processing speed of a job. We'll delve into the main options in this chapter.

Monitoring Resources

Before we look at options that optimise the way SAS performs, we should look at how SAS can monitor the resources it is using. With good monitoring in place, it becomes easy to see where and what the bottlenecks are, and to measure the effects of any changes being made.

We will only cover the resource-monitoring options that come with SAS here, not the monitoring options offered by the various platforms SAS can run on.

FULLSTIMER

SET AS: SYSTEM OPTION

The SAS System provides the FULLSTIMER option, which triggers the collection of performance figures for each DATA and procedure step and places them in the SAS log.

This option is useful for identifying which steps in your SAS job should be targeted for optimisation, and to monitor the effect of changes you make. It is also useful to identify the bottlenecks: the reasons why your process is prevented from going faster.

By default, SAS uses the STIMER option and displays two metrics after each step: the CPU and real (elapsed) times. Enabling the FULLSTIMER option triggers the display of additional information, such as the amount of memory used. SAS ports for operating systems generate different FULLSTIMER figures. See the SAS host-specific documentation for the exact statistics offered.

FULLSTIMER Output

A sample of a FULLSTIMER output under UNIX is listed below:

```
real time                    0.01 seconds
user cpu time                0.00 seconds
system cpu time              0.00 seconds
Memory                       236k
OS Memory                    6,000.00k
Timestamp                    Friday, 21 June 2013 14:43:47
Page Faults                          3
Page Reclaims                        24
Page Swaps                           0
Voluntary Context Switches           11
Involuntary Context Switches         1
Block Input Operations               2
Block Output Operations              0
```

☞ Under Windows, the FULLSTIMER output only includes the first six lines.

☞ Under Z/OS, the FULLSTIMER option is used in conjunction with the MEMRPT and STATS options.

Here's what the different headings in the above FULLSTIMER output mean.

Real Time

This is the elapsed time, or "wall clock" time: How long we spend waiting for an operation (a step) to complete.

User CPU Time

This is the time spent by the processor to execute code coming from the SAS application. This code is not our program as such; the operating system means "user" from its own perspective. In other words, it is all the SAS System code that was executed to run your job, except for the System Code (see next definition).

System CPU Time

This is the time spent by the processor to execute operating system tasks that support user code, such as reading a disk.

☞ The user CPU time and system CPU time are complementary. The sum of the two is what SAS actually uses to execute the requested task.

☞ Starting with SAS 9, some procedures can use multiple threads. This means that on computers with multiple CPUs, SAS can use several CPUs concurrently. As a result, CPU time can exceed real time in the FULLSTIMER output.

For example, if two CPUs have been used at 100% for 10 seconds of real time, CPU Time will be 20 seconds.

Memory
This is the amount of memory that was used to run a given step.

OS Memory
This is the total amount of operating system memory (RAM) that is available to SAS during a given step. It doesn't represent the entire amount of memory that the SAS session takes up, as SAS overhead activities (SAS manager, etc.) aren't reflected here. Nonetheless, OS Memory is what actually matters for our purposes: looking at a given tasks' resource consumption.

Timestamp
This is the date and time that a step was executed.

Page Faults
This is the number of virtual memory pages that SAS tried to access from memory, but could not, and required an I/O operation to retrieve. This count can also be called 'cache misses'.

Page Reclaims
This is the number of virtual memory pages that could be read from the memory cache and did not require an I/O operation to retrieve. This measure is also called 'cache hits'.

Page Swaps
This is the number of times a process was swapped out of main memory. This occurs when SAS requests more system memory (RAM) than is available and the disk is then used as memory. Paging is better than aborting a job for lack of memory, but disks are much slower than RAM and paging dramatically reduces performance. This is a strong indicator for us to look at ways of optimising the process, either by increasing the available memory, reducing memory requirements or prompting SAS to use its efficient utility files in place of paging.

Voluntary Context Switches
This is the number of times a process releases its CPU time-slice voluntarily before the time-slice allocation has expired. This usually occurs when the process needs an external resource, typically when the CPU waits for an I/O call for more data.

Involuntary Context Switches
This is the number of times a process releases its CPU time-slice involuntarily. This usually happens when its CPU time-slice has expired before the task was finished, or a higher priority task takes its time-slice away.

Block Input Operations
This is the number of I/O operations executed to read data from disk to memory. Not all reads have to utilize an I/O operation since the page being requested may still be cached in memory from previous reads.

Block Output Operations
This is the number of I/O operations executed to write data from memory to disk. These are equivalent to Block Input Operations except that they pertain to writing data to files. As with Block Input Operations, not all block outputs will cause an I/O operation since some pages may be cached in memory before being written.

Interpretation

If your process takes too much time to run, it's usually because it places too much strain on one or more of the following resources:

- CPU
- Memory
- I/O subsystem (permanent storage, whether local or networked)

By examining the FULLSTIMER figures, we can quickly get an idea of what is going on.

Here are some basic general rules for interpreting these figures:

CPU Time vs. Real Time.

In a single CPU setup, if CPU Time is close to Real Time, the CPU is crunching data as fast as it can and is a limiting factor for the job's speed. The benchmark for multi-CPU setups is more complicated. We need to divide the CPU time by number of cores used; if this time is close to Real Time then the CPU is the bottleneck. In both cases having a faster CPU would likely speed up our job

If in contrast, Real Time is much greater than CPU time, the CPU is not working all the time, but rather is waiting for data; the problem lies elsewhere in the system. If the job is the only job running on the machine, this typically means the CPU is waiting for data. Otherwise, the CPU may simply be used by other processes and your job has to wait for its turn, in which case more CPUs may help. If you have this figure available on your operating system, looking at Involuntary Context Switches will tell you more.

Involuntary Context Switches

If the CPU is often interrupted from processing your job, it is a sign that it is under heavy load and your job is competing with other jobs for its share of CPU time.

Memory

If the job uses a large quantity of memory (in relation to how much memory the system has, or how much SAS is allowed to use), this might indicate an area for further investigation of either the job's way of doing things or its memory allocation.

Page Swaps

A high Page Swap count will dramatically slow down your job, and indicates that your job in its current form needs more memory than it is getting in order to be processed efficiently.

Page Reclaims

The higher this number, the better. Any data retrieved in memory rather than on disk (whether for reading or writing) will be retrieved must faster.

Page Faults

Conversely, when SAS tries to find data in the memory cache but eventually has to retrieve it on disk, time is wasted. Firstly because as we know well by now, disk access is much slower than memory access. Secondly, a small amount of time was spent scanning the cache for data that wasn't there.

These metrics can help find the bottlenecks in your SAS processes so you can try and alleviate them. If more information is needed, many tools are available to a system administrator. These can help investigating further how the machine's resources are utilised and pinpoint areas where the machine may be stressed.

Generally, SAS uses very large amounts of data, and the I/O subsystem is the first to require optimisation, so that the data can be transferred in a prompt fashion. Cache misses allow a glimpse into how well the I/Os are performing, but other metrics such as queue length (which measures how many requests are queued and waiting for the I/O subsystem to execute them) should also be used, which are not available in the FULLSTIMER output.

STIMEFMT

SET AS: SYSTEM OPTION

The output from the FULLSTIMER option (as well as from the default, less complete, STIMER option) can be controlled using the STIMEFMT option.

This option controls display parameters such as the time and date formats, separating commas and units. It also controls the contents of option FULLSTIMER's output.

To get syntax help, type:

```
options stimefmt = fmt;
```

and/or

```
options stimefmt = opt;
```

With this, the full list of options is displayed in the log.

Here is an example of how option STIMEFMT can be used:

```
options stimefmt = (tsfull nldatm. memfull kb c e );
```

Under Windows, the above statement displays:

- The time stamp and format it
- Memory consumption in KB with separating commas
- Addition counters

This syntax generates this information:

```
real time          0.01 seconds
user cpu time      0.00 seconds
```

```
system cpu time      0.00 seconds
memory               153.32k
OS Memory            6,000.00k
Timestamp                 Friday, 21 June 2016 15:07:26
Threads      Created          0
Events       Created          0
Locks        Created          0
Memory Pools Created         16
Memory Pools Destroyed       16
```

Get to know the STIMEFMT option and you can easily extract the relevant information from your log.

The LOGPARSE Macro

Lastly, while still on the topic of monitoring the log, we'll mention a very handy tool even though it is not a SAS option. The LOGPARSE macro unsurprisingly parses log files whilst also storing a wealth of performance information metrics in a data set. This data set can be used to programmatically report the performance of all executed jobs. The information stored goes beyond pure performance metrics and includes items such as program and step names and the number of observations processed in a step.

The LOGPARSE macro requires SAS version 9.1.3 or later, can be run on any platform and can read log files from any platform; we can generate our log files on one platform and report on these files on another platform.

The LOGPARSE macro can be downloaded from the SAS Institute web site.

This macro is very useful as is, and we can only hope that it is a precursor to an upcoming full end-of-run log summary for interactive runs.

✋ Please SAS Institute: Give us a way to generate an optionally interactive log analysis report after a run.

Moving Data: Data Set Buffers

While SAS can read data from many sources such as SPDS, relational databases (RDBMS) like DB2 or Teradata, or MDDB cubes, most of the data usually used by SAS jobs is stored in SAS data sets. Therefore, efficient access to SAS data sets is a key to efficient processes. Here we'll examine a few options control how data in data sets is accessed.

The peculiarity of SAS jobs

An essential point about the way SAS uses data must be made here. Please read the hardware chapter if some concepts used in these explanations are foreign.

SAS has a data usage pattern different than what administrators of transactional (OLTP) systems are used to. While most of these systems make a large number of small I/O requests, SAS typically does a small number of large I/O requests. Furthermore, a typical SAS job consists of large sequential requests whereas a typical database workload consists of small random operations.

Sequential access is often common in the day time when users run queries on de-normalised tables, where data access usually consists of few, large and sequential read requests.

At night, when data is refreshed, data usage is more varied, and some jobs will be accessing data sequentially in read mode or in write mode, while other jobs will access data in a more random manner.

Even if most SAS data usage is habitually sequential, it is worth noting that when several users concurrently access a large data set, the access request to that data will appear to be random to the storage subsystem, even if each request is sequential. Similarly some SAS processes such as OLAP queries or queries relying on indexes are more random than sequential in nature.

SAS's mostly sequential and large-volume-based patterns matters for two reasons. The first one is that the performance of storage subsystems used by OLTP systems is traditionally measured in I/O per second or IOPS. In contrast, it is the sustained sequential throughput rate for large data volumes that matters most for typical SAS data storage systems. The other impact of this difference in behaviour is the way the page cache is used. The cache-miss rate can be lower for sequential accesses than for random ones, but the caching mechanism's overhead can become a hindrance when the amount of sequential data accessed at once is greater than the cache size and no data element is accessed twice.

Now that we understand how SAS data sets are used, let's look at the options that impact the way SAS data sets are read and written. These options significantly alter the way SAS data sets are accessed, and have a profound impact on performance.

It is possible to decide how large a data set's atomic data block (or "page") is, how many of them are used to access data, and whether the operating system's caching mechanism is by-passed or not.

BUFSIZE

SET AS: SYSTEM OPTION, DATA SET OPTION

This option fixes a data set's page size at the time the data is created. The page size is a permanent attribute of the data set and is used whenever the data set is accessed for either reading or writing.

A page is the minimum amount of data that can be transferred for a single I/O operation. In other words, a SAS data is divided into pages which all have a size of BUFSIZE. A page contains the data that SAS moves between external storage and memory in a single I/O operation.

This page size can be set globally via the BUFSIZE system option. It can also be set for each individual data set by specifying the BUFSIZE data set option. The data set option takes precedence over the system option. By default BUFSIZE is set to a value of zero, meaning that the

SAS engine is free to pick an appropriate value when the data set is created. Note that it does so by considering observation length, but not the number of observations.

Depending on the host platform, BUFSIZE can be set between 1 kB and 2 GB, though these extremes are usually inefficient.

☞A larger page size can speed up execution time by reducing the number of times SAS has to read from or write to the storage medium. However there is a downside; the improvement in I/O efficiency comes at the cost of increased memory consumption. This means that memory-intensive tasks can be adversely affected by a large page size.

☞ Where a data set is accessed purely in a random manner and one observation at a time, such as when indexes are used, a page large enough to contain just one observation can be the most efficient since only the required data is retrieved. This example is given to emphasise that setting the optimum page size depends on several factors, including record length, data set size and how the data is used.

☞ If you use the COPY procedure to copy a data set to another library that is allocated with a different engine, any specified page size of the data set will not be retained.

☞ You can find the page size for a data set in the output of the CONTENTS procedure, or if you are lucky enough to be using the Display Manager rather than SAS Enterprise Guide, you can right-click on a data set to open the contextual menu, then click on Properties, and finally choose the Details tab.

☞ Under 32 bits Windows, SAS usually picks a page size of 4, 8, 12, or 16 kB. If the observation length exceeds 16 kB, SAS increases the page size in 512-byte increments to allow the observation to fit in a page. Using a multiple of 8 kB is recommended.

BUFNO

SET AS: SYSTEM OPTION, DATA SET OPTION

The BUFNO option determines the number of input/output buffers (data set pages) that SAS uses for transferring data during processing. The number of buffers is not a permanent attribute of a data set; rather it is valid only for the current SAS session or step. The BUFNO option applies to SAS data sets regardless of whether they are opened for input, output, or update.

The number of pages used can be set globally via the BUFNO system option and can be set as needed upon data set access by specifying the BUFNO data set option. As usual, the data set option takes precedence over the system option.

☞ Increasing BUFNO may improve performance by reducing I/O. However, like BUFSIZE this comes at the cost of increased memory usage. When a data set is opened, some system memory is reserved for accessing that data set. The reserved memory is BUFSIZE x BUFNO in size and is not available to other applications or SAS procedures. It's reserved purely for transferring data to or from that data set.

☞ Under 32 bits Windows, the maximum file buffer size is 64 MB, which means that BUFNO times BUFSIZE must be less than 64 MB. For 64-bit Windows systems and Windows on Itanium, the maximum file buffer size is 2 GB.

ALIGNSASIOFILES

SET AS: SYSTEM OPTION AT STARTUP

While we are discussing data set pages, a recently added option is worth mentioning. This option aligns the size of the data set header (which contains the metadata) with the size of the data pages as defined by the BUFSIZE option. By default the header page size is 1 kB on Windows and 8 kB on Unix. The ALIGNSASIOFILES system option forces the header page to be the same size as the data pages.

This option appeared in version 9.3 and its intent is for the data set page boundaries to be aligned with disk cluster boundaries. This permits efficient I/O operations since a request for one dataset page will not fall between 2 disk clusters, which would lead to two disk I/O operations. Good alignment is hard to achieve if the data set header is smaller than the other pages. This potential misalignment is becoming an issue as data storage evolves: on one hand data sets and data set pages grow in size, while on the other hand disks and disk clusters also grow in size. Since the data set headers have remained rather smaller, misalignment has become more common.

The disadvantage of aligning pages is that a bit of disk space is wasted, but this is negligible except for very small data sets, and the potential benefits are worth it. I must admit that I haven't spent a lot of time studying this option. So while I haven't found an example where this made a measurable difference, there may well be good examples of tangible benefits out there. In any case, you may want to enable this sensible option by default unless your data sets are small and disk space is at a premium.

Direct Input/Output Preamble

Before we examine the direct I/O options, we must understand how the operating system file cache works. You may want to read the section about caching in chapter 3 if the concept is not familiar.

File caching mechanisms generally works well and all operating systems now implement it. However there are cases when it does not provide any performance gain. If the files read are so large that they cannot fit in memory and each piece of data is only accessed once (such as when a very large data set is sequentially read or written), the caching system brings no benefit. Similarly, if many users access many files, the cache available for each file may become too small to be useful. Finally if a large file is accessed in a totally random manner and no data is accessed more than once, caching is of no benefit either.

In these cases, caching data lowers the data throughput rate well below its potential. This is because caching involves a number of overheads for moving data between the disk, the cache, and the application. One overhead is that read-aheads lengthen all reads. Other overheads include: scanning the cache in order to find out whether a disk access is required, managing the cache's contents, and deciding what to cache and what to stop caching. In cases where caching will not bring benefits, avoiding these overheads accelerates data transfers considerably. This is made all the truer given those cases usually involve large amounts of data,

This is where direct Input/Output (detailed below) becomes an interesting choice. Simply put, it is a way SAS provides to completely bypass the operating system file cache. An ideal scenario for using direct I/O would be a job sequentially accessing different data sets which are all larger than the file cache.

☞ Selectively bypassing the cache for processes where it is counter-productive is doubly beneficial. It not only speeds up these processes, it will also speed up those processes which do use the cache, as the cache will not be swamped by unused data.

Direct Input/Output Option under Windows: SGIO

SET AS: SYSTEM OPTION, DATA SET OPTION

In the Windows world, the SAS option to enable direct I/O is called SGIO, which stands for "Scatter-read/Gather-write Input Output." This option can be set globally as a system option, or can be set for each individual data set at the time of use by specifying the SGIO data set option. As usual, the data set option takes precedence over the system option. Using the SGIO option instructs SAS to bypass the operating system file cache and to access the storage subsystem directly.

Under the Windows operating environment, if the SGIO system option is set, the maximum number of bytes that can be processed in an I/O operation is 64MB.
Therefore, number-of-buffers times page-size ≤ 64MB.

Direct Input/Output Options under Unix

In the UNIX world, several options control direct I/O:

- The libname option ENABLEDIRECTIO
- The libname option USEDIRECTIO
- The data set option USEDIRECTIO
- The libname option TRANSFERSIZE

The ENABLEDIRECTIO option in the LIBNAME statement enables direct I/O for all data sets in a library. By itself, using the ENABLEDIRECTIO option does not turn on direct I/O processing. However, without it no direct I/O will take place regardless of other options.

The actual triggering of direct I/O is done by using the USEDIRECTIO option, either in the LIBNAME statement or as a data set option.

The additional option TRANSFERSIZE used in the LIBNAME statement specifies the size of the data buffer used to transfer data to or from disk during direct I/O operations. There has been no guidance from SAS as to why the TRANSFERSIZE option was created, rather than simply using BUFNO and BUFSIZE as SGIO does by default. However do note that since TRANSFERSIZE takes for parameter a numeric value that defines the transfer buffer size, it should accordingly be set to a multiple of BUFSIZE (the data set page size).

Data Set Buffer Case Studies

Each case is different and ideally tests should be conducted in order to decide upon the values of BUFSIZE and BUFNO as well as to decide when to use direct I/O. These decisions will depend on the hardware, the data, how the data is used, and what other jobs are running. The following test is however as an example of the great impact changing the default data set parameters has.

Below are data sets of various sizes created by writing data sequentially while varying the values of BUFSIZE, BUFNO, and SGIO on a PC running 32bit Windows XP.

No other jobs were running. Here are the elapsed times in seconds. The first row uses the default SAS settings. The best times are underlined, and the grey zones are where enabling SGIO slowed down the data transfer compared to just using the default.

Table 5.1: Run times for various values of BUFSIZE, BUFNO and SGIO for a 100 MB data set

100,000 kB		BUFNO				
		1	5	25	100	500
BUFSIZE	SGIO					
0	no	1.96	.	.	.	.
4k	no	2.41	2.62	1.66	1.65	1.67
	yes	9.62	6.09	1.55	1.18	1.39
8k	no	2.19	1.13	1.68	1.22	1.25
	yes	5.40	3.20	1.19	1.02	0.45
16k	no	1.04	1.04	2.77	1.15	2.60
	yes	3.18	1.91	0.62	1.09	0.38
32k	no	1.93	1.81	0.94	1.97	0.93
	yes	2.16	1.42	0.91	0.79	0.42
64k	no	1.86	0.89	2.96	1.01	1.27
	yes	0.82	1.96	0.96	0.71	.
128k	no	0.89	1.09	1.06	3.30	1.23
	yes	1.22	0.99	0.38	0.40	.

Table 5.2: Run times for various values of BUFSIZE, BUFNO and SGIO for a 300 MB data set

300,000 kB		BUFNO				
		1	5	25	100	500
BUFSIZE	**SGIO**					
0	no	3.98	.	.	.	.
4k	no	5.32	4.83	4.94	5.03	5.47
	yes	28.97	17.03	4.80	2.56	1.67
8k	no	3.18	3.48	3.43	3.55	3.34
	yes	15.54	7.67	2.77	1.67	2.33
16k	no	3.00	3.23	2.89	2.89	2.82
	yes	7.62	4.43	2.75	1.39	1.90
32k	no	3.86	4.48	2.73	2.77	2.78
	yes	3.91	2.81	1.54	1.20	1.75
64k	no	2.80	3.95	4.00	3.73	3.70
	yes	2.68	2.01	1.34	1.29	.
128k	no	6.73	4.80	3.56	4.51	3.14
	yes	2.04	1.48	1.33	1.24	.

Table 5.3: Run times for various values of BUFSIZE, BUFNO and SGIO for a 1,000 MB data set

1,000,000 kB		BUFNO				
		1	5	25	100	500
BUFSIZE	**SGIO**					
0	no	17.37	.	.	.	.
4k	no	17.22	16.63	17.02	17.36	18.02
	yes	117.02	58.31	15.71	8.65	9.04
8k	no	11.55	11.35	11.44	11.59	11.39
	yes	52.57	28.23	10.19	7.53	6.96
16k	no	11.80	10.89	9.79	9.48	9.60
	yes	26.79	14.44	6.47	6.44	8.46
32k	no	9.48	10.93	11.35	10.03	11.15
	yes	13.55	10.22	6.54	6.75	8.40
64k	no	16.23	14.11	10.00	13.97	17.58
	yes	8.40	6.98	8.26	6.32	.
128k	no	17.81	11.32	12.87	15.92	9.95
	yes	6.55	6.08	7.95	8.10	.

Table 5.4: Run times for various values of BUFSIZE, BUFNO and SGIO for a 3,000 MB data set

3,000,000 kB		BUFNO				
		1	5	25	100	500
BUFSIZE	SGIO					
0	no	41.59	.	.	.	.
4k	no	55.60	55.06	55.05	56.02	55.29
	yes	353.42	172.07	47.39	28.17	27.88
8k	no	36.77	37.14	37.98	37.17	36.97
	yes	158.94	81.27	28.75	25.23	23.73
16k	no	33.89	32.52	34.17	32.70	32.38
	yes	79.27	43.33	22.17	23.34	22.47
32k	no	36.82	37.27	37.55	36.79	39.38
	yes	42.51	27.91	20.52	21.17	20.23
64k	no	43.61	42.90	37.64	38.23	41.14
	yes	25.58	20.74	19.68	21.20	.
128k	no	42.66	36.59	40.59	39.06	41.19
	yes	20.07	21.20	19.07	19.15	.

Table 5.5: Run times for various values of BUFSIZE, BUFNO and SGIO for a 10,000 MB data set

10,000,000 kB		BUFNO				
		1	5	25	100	500
BUFSIZE	SGIO					
0	no	195.45	.	.	.	.
4k	no	235.25	236.25	235.56	239.78	235.39
	yes	1177.55	572.32	157.28	93.60	93.96
8k	no	163.77	162.05	164.22	164.05	161.34
	yes	542.85	268.86	95.45	81.07	80.84
16k	no	138.03	140.26	136.16	137.49	136.11
	yes	265.46	142.55	75.28	74.61	81.70
32k	no	143.70	148.85	137.96	147.67	143.98
	yes	140.56	93.84	73.35	73.33	75.48
64k	no	180.47	171.39	166.63	151.69	173.16
	yes	88.62	70.14	71.62	72.00	.
128k	no	235.25	236.25	235.56	239.78	235.39
	yes	70.72	71.30	71.34	70.33	.

The missing values are due to a process failing as the result of an I/O error. These I/O errors were constant when using SGIO for the 2 largest buffer sizes of 500x64kB=32,000 kB and 500x128kB=64,000 kB, even though these values are under the 64 MB limit that Windows can normally accept.

Several comments come to mind when looking at these results.

- It is easily possible to improve on the default settings and speed up sequential accesses significantly.
  Memory is not a commodity that SAS makes enough use of, and this can be to our disadvantage. Setting more aggressively large buffering parameters when sequentially accessing large tables pays back a dividend in the form of drastically reduced run times.
- The best results are always achieved when the value of BUFSIZE is not small. In this case, 16 kB or more works as a rule of thumb.
- The value of BUFNO has less impact, although smaller values still perform worse than larger ones.
- While the BUFNO and BUFSIZE values must be high, we need balance. Setting both too high is counter-productive. In fact we can observe that large values have a decreasing return while 25 x 32 kB seems to be something of a sweet spot in these tests.
- The fastest times were always achieved when using SGIO. This task is purely sequential and using direct I/O yields sizeable performance gains ranging from a factor of 1/2 to a factor of 1/5th compared to the default SAS settings. This is even true for a small 100 MB table.
- The slowest times were also achieved when using SGIO. These bad results take place when the buffer is too small. Remember that SGIO is not a silver bullet. Learn your data, learn your processes, and optimise your settings accordingly.

☞ As an informal observation, I have noticed that direct I/O can advantageously be used more often with Solid State Drives than with Hard Disk Drives, probably because SSDs have a much lower latency than HDDs, and therefore benefit less from the operating system cache.

Moving Data: Other Buffers

Moving data is a central theme of SAS jobs', and more options exist to optimize the way disks or networks transport data.

IBUFSIZE

SET AS: SYSTEM OPTION

Just as SAS needs memory space as a "port hole" to access data from data sets, SAS needs memory space to read data from indexes. SAS automatically allocates a minimal number of buffers in order to navigate the index file. This option is a system option, and sets an index's page size at the time of the index creation.

Typically, you do not need to specify the index page size. However, the following situations could require a larger page size than the default:

The number of pages required to store the index file varies with the page size, the length of the index value, and the cardinality of the values. Increasing the page size allows more index values to be stored on each page, thus reducing the number of levels in the index. The more levels, the longer the index search takes.

The main resource that is saved when reducing levels in the index is the number of I/O operations. If an application is experiencing many I/O operations on the index file, increasing the page size can help.

☞ The index file structure requires a minimum of three index values to be stored on a page. If the length of an index value is very large, you can get an error message indicating that the index could not be created because the page size is too small to hold three index values. Increasing page size will eliminate this error.

☞ An index file must be recreated after increasing IBUFSIZE system option.

☞ As for the data set buffer options, experimentation is the best way to determine an optimal index page size.

IBUFNO
SET AS: SYSTEM OPTION

This option is similar to the BUFNO option, but is used for index files. Typically, we don't need to specify extra buffers, however using IBUFNO= to specify extra buffers can improve execution time by limiting the number of input/output operations that are required for a particular index file. Again, the improvement in execution time comes at the expense of increased memory consumption.

VBUFSIZE and OBSBUF
SET AS: SYSTEM OPTION (VBUFSIZE), VIEW OPTION (OBSBUF)

Like the other buffer options, these two options reserve a block of main memory, in this case to set the size of the output buffers used by DATA step views.

These two options differ slightly from previous buffer options as VBUFSIZE sets the buffer size in number of bytes while OBSBUF sets the buffer size in number of observations. Another difference is that VBUFSIZE is a system option while OBSBUF is used when the view is referenced.

Here are two examples:

```
option vbufsize=32767;                /* Set a 32 kB buffer  */

proc print data=VIEW22(obsbuf=5000);  /* Set a 5k obs buffer */
run;
```

☞ OBSBUF takes precedence over VBUFSIZE.

☞ View buffer size is not stored as part of a view's metadata. It is set at run time.

TBUFSIZE and TCPMSGLEN

SET AS: SYSTEM OPTION, SIGNON OPTION (TBUFSIZE)

SET AS: SYSTEM OPTION IN CONFIG FILE (TCPMSGLEN)

While we are looking at moving data faster by using large buffers, and for the sake of comprehensiveness, the options TBUFSIZE and TCPMSGLEN need mentioning. They set the size of the transfer buffers when SAS transfers data between a client and a server across a network.

The default values are normally fine, but if you experience slow speeds or have large amounts of data to transfer, increasing the default values can improve performance. It does so by reducing the number of calls that the application layer makes to the communications layer for a data transfer. Other factors such as the amount of data and network bandwidth must be considered to optimize buffer performance.

Here is how these buffers are used:

Figure 5.1: SAS/CONNECT buffers

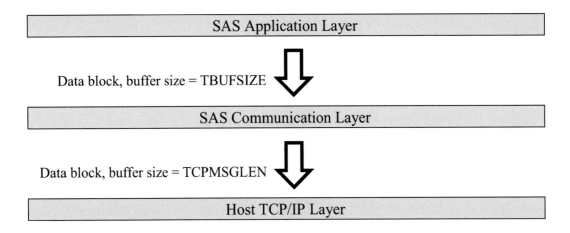

TBUFSIZE sets the buffer size for the SAS Application Layer. The default value for TBUFSIZE is 32 kB. TBUFSIZE is only specified in the client session.

TCPMSGLEN sets the buffer size for the SAS Communication Layer. That's the size of the TCP data buffers that will be transferred between client and server. It can be specified in both sessions and the smaller value is used if they differ. The default value for TCPMSGLEN is 32 kB except for Windows where it is 16 kB.

The SAS Communication Layer transfers the entire buffer it receives if TCPMSGLEN is of the same size as TBUFSIZE, or divides the data into multiple transfers if TCPMSGLEN is smaller than TBUFSIZE.

Managing Memory

SAS does not have a view of what the OS does with the computer's memory. SAS can only request memory –we call this memory virtual memory– and the OS allocates either RAM or paging space depending on availability. So the options below are here to indicate to SAS what we expect the OS will do. They are not options that can drive the OS's behaviour, or that describe the actual behaviour.

MEMSIZE

SET AS: SYSTEM OPTION AT STARTUP

This option sets the maximum amount of virtual memory that the SAS session is allowed to use. Virtual memory is the sum of RAM space and paging space made available by the OS.

☞ MEMSIZE=0 can also be written as MEMSIZE=MAX. Do not use this value in multi-user environments.

☞ SAS will not allocate the amount of memory set by the MEMSIZE option right away, but will allocate it as required up to the value of MEMSIZE.

☞ Once the SAS is started, the value of MEMSIZE cannot be changed, the SAS session will have to live with the chosen value.

Two things should be considered:

The value MAX is only optimal if SAS is the only process running on the machine and if only one user uses SAS. In other cases, one SAS process might allocate too much memory on the machine and prevent the other processes from running properly. Do not use this value on Unix machines or on multi-user machines.

Setting a high value may lead to some data being paged out to disk. This in turn may have a greater negative impact on process speed than setting a lower value for MEMSIZE. On the other hand, a high value might allow a process to complete, albeit slowly if paging is used.

☞ 32-bit OSes are limited to an address space of 4GB, of which the OS often uses at least 1 GB. 32-bit Windows contains a further limitation: individual applications cannot use more than 2 GB of virtual space unless a special switch is used at start-up.

REALMEMSIZE

SET AS: SYSTEM OPTION AT STARTUP

Real memory means RAM space only, not paging space. This option sets the maximum amount of real memory that some procedures can expect to allocate. Remember, you can't know what the OS will do. This value is only here for SAS to tune its programs. The default value is 0 (zero), which again allows SAS to choose a reasonable value depending on the amount of physical memory available at the time SAS is started.

On single-user machines, the value should be lower than the amount of real memory available once the OS and the other applications have taken what they need.

On multi-user machines, active processes should ideally not page. In this case, the value should be close to that of MEMSIZE.

Bigger is not always better. The SAS 9.4 documentation for PROC SORT states:

"You can experiment with the REALMEMSIZE value until you reach optimum performance for your environment. In some cases, optimum performance can be achieved with a very low REALMEMSIZE value. A low value could cause SAS to use less memory and leave more memory for the operating system to perform I/O caching."

Unfortunately, there is a bit of confusion as to which procedures use this option. The documentation mentions that it is used by procedures that can use both memory and utility disk space, such as PROC SUMMARY and PROC SORT. This would make sense as REALMEMSIZE would be the limit at which paging starts. Technical support tells me that it is only multithreaded procedures which use the option. In version 9.4, I checked that PROC TABULATE does use REALMEMSIZE and doesn't use utility files. As such, it seems the 9.4 documentation may be wrong or out of date in which case, the procedures impacted are the so-called Scalable SAS procedures.

In version 9.4, the scalable procedures are:

Base SAS: SORT, SUMMARY, MEANS, REPORT, TABULATE, and SQL

SAS/STAT: GLM, LOESS, REG, ROBUSTREG.

Enterprise Miner: DMREG, DMINE

XMRLMEM

THIS OPTION CANNOT BE SET, ONLY QUERIED

Whenever REALMEMSIZE has been set to zero and you want to know how much memory SAS can allocate, use the undocumented XMRLMEM option:

```
%put Free RAM =
    %sysfunc(putn(%sysfunc(getoption(xmrlmem))/1024**2,comma10.))MB;
```

This option's value matches the value of REALMEMSIZE at startup, and dynamically changes to show available memory depending on SAS's usage.

You can also use it anytime to see how much memory SAS has left to use. This comes handy when using in-memory data (see a few pages further).

SUMSIZE

SET AS: SYSTEM OPTION, PROCEDURE OPTION (FOR PROC MEANS)

This option sets the maximum amount of real memory (RAM) that some data summation procedures are free to use.

The SUMSIZE option affects these procedures: MEANS, OLAP, REPORT, SUMMARY, SURVEYFREQ, SURVEYLOGISTIC, SURVEYMEANS and TABULATE.

While too little memory being available can adversely affect SAS performance, making large amounts of memory available can be of no benefit. The key for determining whether additional memory might improve performance is whether the summarization fits in memory.

If the procedure requires more memory than it is allowed, the procedure will page to disk, which means it will store on disk data that would normally go in memory, thereby slowing the process down.

Summary

It is important we understand how memory option settings interact with, and affect each other:

MEMSIZE limits how much Memory + Page space SAS can use.

REALMEMSIZE is a subset of MEMSIZE and limits how much memory SAS can use.

SUMSIZE (or SORTSIZE) sets how much real memory a procedure is allowed to use; this cannot exceed the overriding value REALMEMSIZE.

Figure 5.2: Scope of the different memory allocation options

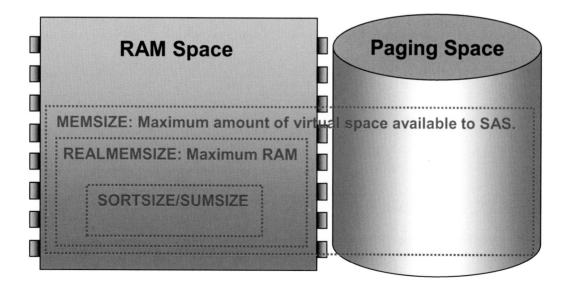

Other memory-related options

More memory-related options, which vary depending on the platform, can be seen by running:

```
proc options group=memory; run;
```

In-memory data

The field of loading data into memory is evolving very fast and is very exciting. As disks struggle to give access to an ever-increasing amount of data and as memory becomes cheaper, it is starting to make economic sense to provide access to data from memory.

MEMLIB

SET AS: SYSTEM OPTION AT STARTUP, LIBNAME OPTION (WINDOWS ONLY)

Do you dream of having multi-GB/s data access speed where the CPU is the only bottleneck when accessing data in the WORK library? If so, author and reader indeed share much in common; not the least item of which is that our dreams have been made quite real by SAS Institute: Option MEMLIB tells SAS that a library is RAM-based.

If invoked as a start-up option, the result is a WORK library that sits in RAM. Obviously, this may not be practicable if we process very large files in the WORK library, but if the data processing in WORK consists of accessing large numbers of small datasets, this option is incredibly valuable. RAM is the fastest type of memory there is. Concordantly, if your data processing pattern allows you to use it, this option can accelerate our processes tremendously.

Write 1 GB in 0.4 seconds, only limited by the CPU: Nice!

```
data TEMP;                      NOTE: DATA statement used (Total process time):
  length X $1018;                     real time         0.37 seconds
  do I=1 to 1e6;                      cpu time          0.37 seconds
    output;
  end;
run;
```

If we use this option within the LIBNAME statement, we can create a library in memory with the same characteristics mentioned above: high speed with an associated risk of filling up available memory. The syntax is slightly odd because we will have to provide an existing physical path for the library which will never be used.

```
libname RAMLIB "c:\" memlib;
```

☞ Unfortunately, this option is only available on the Windows platform at the time of writing.

☞ 32 bits Windows limits individual applications to no more than 2 GB of memory space overall, unless a special switch is used at start-up.

☞ If you want to keep the data created in your RAM libraries, don't forget to copy it to a permanent library before ending your SAS session.

☞ When you no longer need your library, make sure to free up the memory by deleting all the files, otherwise the data will stay in memory. We can do this from within SAS by running this program:

```
proc datasets lib=RAMLIB kill nolist;
quit;
libname RAMLIB clear;
```

✋ Please SAS Institute: Provide this option on other platforms.

MEMMAXSZ

SET AS: SYSTEM OPTION AT STARTUP (WINDOWS ONLY)

This option specifies the maximum amount of memory to allocate for memory-based libraries. The memory allocated by MEMMAXSZ is outside of the REALMEMSIZE allocation.

See the diagram at the end of this section to see how the options used to size memory usage are interacting.

MEMBLKSZ

SET AS: SYSTEM OPTION AT STARTUP (WINDOWS ONLY)

This option sets the memory block size for RAM-based libraries. The value of the MEMBLKSZ system option defines the amount of memory that is initially allocated.

Additional memory can be allocated as needed in multiples of MEMBLKSZ up to the amount of memory that is specified in the MEMMAXSZ option.

MEMCACHE

SET AS: SYSTEM OPTION (WINDOWS ONLY)

Another way to load data in the memory is the MEMCACHE option. This option allows us to use the memory available to SAS as a SAS-controlled file cache. The data will be loaded in the cache as it is written to disk.

The Operating System's caching mechanism also does this, but you can never be sure exactly what will be cached. As a result, the data we want to keep in memory may not be there when we need it.

There are three states MEMCACHE can be in:

- MEMCACHE = 4 : CACHE ON. Specifies that memory cache is on. Data written to disk will also be saved in the cache.

☞ Note that the data read from disk will not be cached. Caching only takes places as the data is written.

- MEMCACHE = 1 : CACHE LOCKED. Specifies to not add any new files to the cache. Read operations to files that are already in the cache continue as long as MEMCACHE is not off. If we overwrite a file already in the cache, it is taken out of the cache.

- MEMCACHE = 0 : CACHE OFF. Specifies that the memory cache is off. Caching no longer occurs. Memory will not be freed.

Example

```
libname MYLIB "c:\temp";

* Start caching. Anything written to disk will be cached in memory;
options memcache = 4;

data MYLIB.DS1(compress=no);
  length X $1016;
  do I = 1 to 1e6;
    output;
  end;
run ;

* Stop caching. Cache is still active, we can read from it;
options memcache = 1;

data _null_;
  set MYLIB.DS1;
run;
```

```
NOTE: There were 1000000 observations read from the data set MYLIB.DS1.
NOTE: DATA statement used (Total process time):
      real time          0.35 seconds
      cpu time           0.32 seconds
```

1 GB read in 0.35 seconds, only limited by the CPU. That's good!

There are serious downsides to the current implementation of the MEMSIZE option, however. Let's have a look.

⌘ Be careful when using MEMCACHE: freeing the cache memory is difficult.

As of version 9.4, the only way to clear the memory used by the SAS cache is either to end the SAS session, or to delete the cached data set while MEMCACHE is set to 4.

Setting option:

```
options memcache = 0;
```

will tell SAS to stop using the cache, but the memory will not be freed. It will remain unavailable to any application until you delete the cached data sets, or until you end SAS.

The SAS documentation states:

"Files in the cache are kept until SAS is shut down, caching is terminated, or more space is required for new files."

This has been confirmed by SAS technical support to be misleading and will be corrected in a future version of the documentation.

⌘ Be careful when using MEMCACHE: data confusion is easy.

Consider the following example:

```
options memcache = 4;        %* enable cache                          ;
data A; X=1; run;            %* load data in cache                    ;

options memcache = 0;        %* disable cache                         ;
data A; X=2; run;            %* refresh data, the cache is untouched  ;

options memcache = 1;        %* read table A from cache               ;
data B; set A; put X=; run;  %* X=1                                   ;

options memcache = 0;        %* read table A from disk                ;
data B; set A; put X=; run;  %* X=2                                   ;
```

We have access to two versions of the same table here: one stored in the cache and one stored on disk. There might exist cases where this is useful, but they are also significant possibilities for confusion and errors. This highlights the need for an easy way to clear cache data.

✋ Please SAS Institute: Provide an option to free memory and delete MEMCACHE data.

SASFILE

SASFILE IS NOT AN OPTION, IT IS A STATEMENT

Since the SASFILE statement allows the loading of data into memory, it is logical to cover it at the same time as the two similar options above. SASFILE is available on all platforms.

Option MEMLIB creates a RAM-based library.

Option MEMCACHE retains dataset data in memory as it's written to disk.

The SASFILE statement allows us to load a dataset into memory. This is very handy when we know that we are going to read the same data several times: it's loaded once and then can access it from memory as needed.

☞ MEMCACHE loads the data as it is written do disk, SASFILE loads the data as it reads it from disk.

The syntax to use SASFILE is very simple:

```
sasfile MYLIB.MYTAB load;    * loads the table in memory;
sasfile MYLIB.MYTAB close;   * unloads the table from memory;
```

There is a third option, open, that is used the same manner:

```
sasfile MYLIB.MYTAB open;
```

This option tells SAS that we want the data to be loaded in memory, but to wait until the first time it is used before the actual loading takes place.

Many restrictions currently exist as to which data can be loaded in memory using the SASFILE statement

☞ One cannot add dataset options after the data set name, the whole dataset has to be loaded as is.

☞ One cannot load a view, only a data set can be loaded.

☞ One cannot load an SPDE table, only a BASE engine data set can be loaded.

✋ Please SAS Institute: Is it possible to make the SASFILE statement even more useful and lift these restrictions in an upcoming version of SAS?

Table 5.6: Comparison of the three methods to load data in memory

Action	MEMLIB	MEMCACHE	SASFILE
How to load data into memory	Write the data normally as you would in any library	1- Set MEMCACHE= 4 2- Write the data normally to your disk library.	Use the SAFILE statement with option load.
How to read data from memory	Read the data normally as you would in any library.	1- Set MEMCACHE to 1 (or keep it to 4 to load more data). 2- Read the data normally as you would in any library.	Read the data normally as you would in any library.
Compression	Compressed data sets stay compressed in memory, saving space.	Compressed data sets stay compressed in memory, saving space	Compressed data sets stay compressed in memory, saving space.
Load partial data	Use the data normally as you would in any library.	Use the data normally as you would in any library	You can only load a complete data set, no options, no views.
Saving data	You must save the data that you want to keep or it will be lost when you close SAS.	The data that was loaded in memory is already on disk	The data that was loaded in memory is already on disk.
How to unload data from memory and free the memory	Delete the library's data sets.	Exit SAS, delete the data sets.	Close SASFILE table.
Options limiting the amount of memory available for in-memory data	MEMMAXSZ , MEMSIZE	MEMMAXSZ , MEMSIZE	MEMSIZE
Event in case of insufficient memory available	An insufficient space error is generated.	No message is generated when more data is processed than can fit in the available memory.	A warning is generated stating the numbers of pages that could be loaded. Subsequent attempts to use the table result in an I/O error until the SASFILE CLOSE statement is run.
Platform	Windows	Windows	All
SPDE data support	No	No	No

Note that the memory used by in-memory data is not affected by the limit set by the REALMEMSIZE option.

The following diagram shows how the various memory options interact.

Figure 5.3: Scope of the in-memory data allocation options

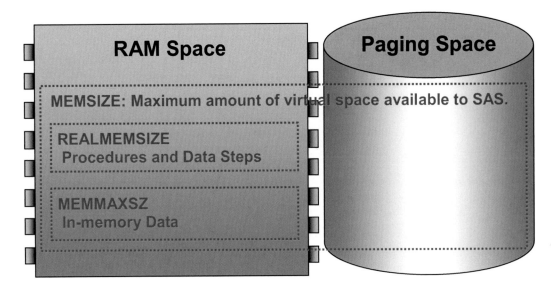

Multi-threading

The option to split certain tasks into separate pieces and to run these pieces in parallel threads was added in version 9 of SAS. Running tasks in parallel can allow them to complete sooner.

THREADS

SET AS: SYSTEM OPTION, PROCEDURE OPTION

The THREADS option enables processes that are thread-enabled to take advantage of multiple CPUs by threading processing and I/O operations. Threading achieves a degree of parallelism that generally reduces the real time to completion at the possible cost of additional CPU resources.

Since SAS 9.0, the thread-enabled processes include:

- Base SAS engine indexing
- Base SAS procedures: SORT, SUMMARY, MEANS, REPORT, TABULATE, and SQL
- SAS/STAT procedures: GLM, LOESS, REG, ROBUSTREG.
- Enterprise Miner procedures: DMREG, DMINE

Since version 9.4, SAS/STAT procedures ADAPTIVEREG, FMM, GLMSELECT, MIXED, QUANTLIFE, QUANTREG, and QUANTSELECT have been added to the list.

We'll have a look at three of these procedure in this chapter, and see how they benefit from multi-threading for a given scenario by scaling the number of CPUs available.

☞ Option NOTHREADS turns off threaded processing.

CPUCOUNT

SET AS: SYSTEM OPTION

Specifies the number of processors that the thread-enabled applications should assume will be available for concurrent processing. The value can be an integer between 1 and 1024, or the word ACTUAL.

Setting CPUCOUNT = ACTUAL causes the option to use the number of logical processors associated with the operating system. If the operating system is executing in a partition, the value of the CPUCOUNT system is the number of processors that are associated with the operating system in that partition. If the processors allow hyper-threading, CPUCOUNT takes this into account.

For multi-threading to be used, the value of CPUCOUNT must be greater than one, and the THREADS option must be set. These 2 options have complementary roles: The option THREADS determines when the threaded processing can be used. The CPUCOUNT option suggests how many CPUs are available for use by thread-enabled SAS procedures.

☞ Option THREADS determines when threaded processing is in effect. The system option CPUCOUNT= suggests how many system CPUs are available for use by thread-enabled SAS processes.

☞ If the THREADS system option is set to NOTHREADS, the CPUCOUNT= option has no effect.

☞ In some cases, for example when processing small data sets, SAS may determine that single-threaded operation is the most efficient.

UTILLOC

SET AS: SYSTEM OPTION AT STARTUP

Some procedures use so-called utility files to store intermediate calculation data when they run out of memory. For example, we have watched our old friend PROC SORT accesses several files during an external sort: the input file, the utility files, and the output (sorted) file. In order to maximise throughput, it is best to spread these so each I/O subsystem only does one thing at a time.

By default, the location for the utility files is the same as the WORK library.

Unless the procedure does not have to use data in the WORK library, this situation can lead to a dramatic drop in the disk throughput as the disk has to alternate between processing requests relative to the utility file and processing requests relative to the data.

By using the UTILLOC option, it is possible to ask SAS to store the utility files elsewhere. The UTILLOC option specifies one or more file system locations in which threaded applications can store utility files.

This avoids contention on the WORK disk since SAS can use data in the WORK library while storing its transitory data on a different disk.

Starting with SAS 9, it is possible to have several locations defined for utility files. These multiple locations can be used by multi-threaded procedures to give each thread a dedicated location for its data. Note that performance will only improve if the different paths are on different I/O devices (drives). Using different paths on the same drive will not help at all.

The multi-threaded procedures that make use of utility files are SORT, SUMMARY, TABULATE and REPORT.

PROC SQL can also benefit from multiple utility paths when it calls the threaded sort utility.

Robert Ray notes in his SUGI 28 paper that in an effort to spread the load, SAS Institute configured PROC SORT to behave differently to other procedures.

This knowledge can help when we **only have 2 paths** to give to the utility files:

"To best leverage multiple utility file paths, the SUMMARY, TABULATE and REPORT procedures currently use the first UTILLOC path for scratch space while the shared threaded sorting utility defaults to the second location."

Therefore, Robert Ray recommends that *"for optimal performance with only two utility paths, SASWORK and UTILLOC path #1 be the same path while UTILLOC path #2 point to a separate I/O device."*

For example:

```
-work "d:"
-utilloc "('d:' 'e: ')"
```

☞ By default, UTILLOC points to the work directory. If your output file is also in the work library, moving the utility file will make a significant difference.

☞ If multiple locations are specified in the UTILLOC parameter, each location is used on a rotating basis.

☞ The UTILLOC= system option affects the placement of the utility files only if multiple threads are used. If multi-threading is not used, then the utility file resides in the work library.

CPUCOUNT Benchmark: PROC SQL

Here we are creating a 10-million row table with 24 variables. They all have the same values, with a cardinality of 100. This benchmark was run on a 16-CPU UNIX machine.

For the first benchmark, we simply join the table onto itself using the union operator and look at memory usage and elapse time. We vary the number of processors from 1 to 16 and the number of observations read in the joined tables from 1 million to 10 million rows.

Figure 5.4: PROC SQL union benchmark, 1 to 16 processors, Elapsed time

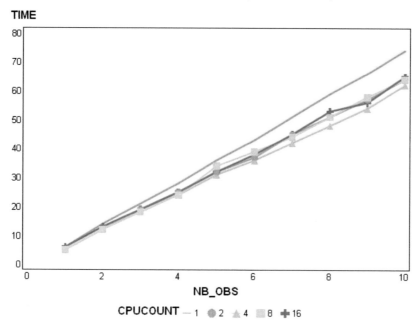

We can see here that the return of adding additional CPUs is not great. While using more than one CPU helps, and the best times are consistently obtained when using four processors, results actually worsen beyond this.

All in all, the speed gains are not great for our test. Let's look at memory usage.

Figure 5.5: PROC SQL union benchmark, 1 to 16 processors, Memory usage

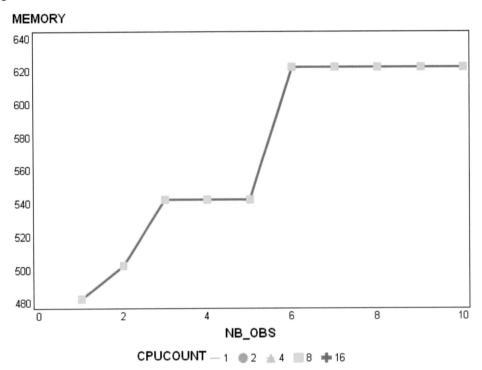

Surprisingly, memory usage doesn't change at all when more threads are used. Interestingly, it seems to increase in steps as observation count increases: 3 to 5 million observations use 540 MB, and then 6 to 10 million rows use 610 MB.

Multithreading hasn't shone too brightly for this particular example. That's because PROC SQL only uses multi-threading to accelerate its `group by` and `order by` clauses.

So let's try sorting now, and use PROC SORT to see how it fares.

CPUCOUNT Benchmark: PROC SORT

Here, we have the same 10-million row table containing 24 variables; we keep adding variables to sort by, increasing the length of the BY statement.

Figure 5.6: PROC SORT benchmark, 1 to 16 processors, Elapsed time

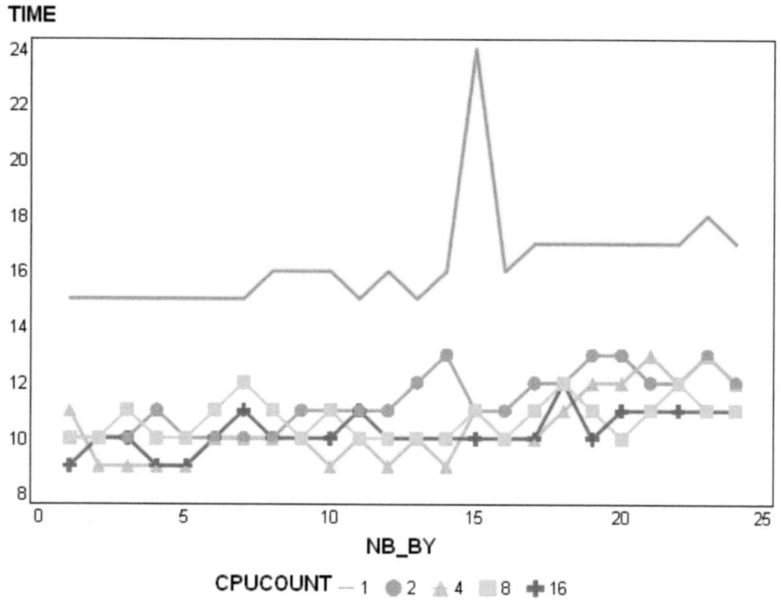

The gains brought about by running multiple threads are much more apparent in this case, especially when going from one to two threads. The number of BY variables doesn't affect processing time much, probably because of the way the data was created. As with the previous test, the best option for this data sample seems to use 4 threads.

Figure 5.7: PROC SORT benchmark, 1 to 16 processors, Memory usage

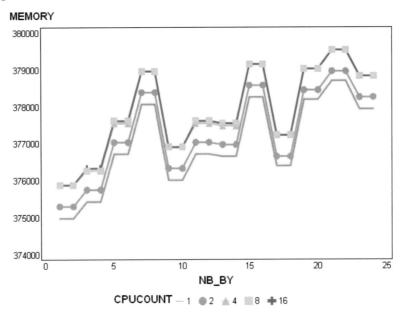

Memory usage is pretty much independent of the number of threads. It is actually also independent of the number of BY variables. Note that it's only because the Y axis is magnified that we can even see visible differences. The pattern as we increase the number of variables is odd but consistent. For more interesting patterns, let's now look at PROC SUMMARY.

CPUCOUNT Benchmark: PROC SUMMARY

Here, we once again use out 10-million row table with 24 variables and we keep adding variables to the class statement until we summarise 24 classes.

Figure 5.8: PROC SUMMARY benchmark, 1 to 16 processors, Elapsed time

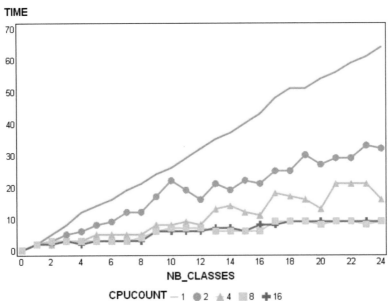

Now, that's more like it! That's the kind of chart that's perfect for a book such as this one, isn't it? Time increases as we add more variables and decreases as we dedicate more processors to our task.

In this case, the gains are dramatic and almost linear at first: doubling the number of threads halves the time taken until we reach 8 threads. Notice the great gains made when using 4 threads and the number of classes is a multiple of 4. We can see a similar (albeit less marked) pattern with 2 threads for multiples of 2 classes and for 8 threads for multiples of 8 classes.

Figure 5.9: PROC SUMMARY benchmark, 1 to 16 processors, Memory usage

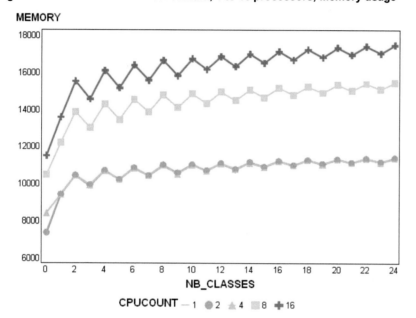

Memory usage remains constant when moving from 1 to 4 threads and then increases significantly when going to 8 and to 16 threads. However, memory usage is hardly affected by the number of class variables. Another obvious and interesting pattern here is how memory usage changes depending on whether the number of classes is odd or even.

In this example, using 4 to 8 threads seem to be the sweet spot for maximum efficiency, depending on available resources.

CPUCOUNT Benchmark: Conclusion

The data we used for these tests is atypical because it needs to be easy to replicate. In the real world, results will depend on hardware and on data as always, but there is no doubt that we can reap significant benefits by using more CPUs to run some of our processes.

There is no doubt that SAS's multi-threading efficiency will further improve as new releases come out. Parallel processing is a maturing field in software engineering and we can look forward to very significant gains as SAS refines and expands upon its relatively new multi-threaded capabilities over time.

Other Options

COMPRESS

SET AS: SYSTEM OPTION, LIBNAME OPTION, DATA SET OPTION

Compressing data sets by using the COMPRESS option is often the easiest way to speed up a process as it reduces the amount of data required to store represent each observation. Hence, enabling compression when creating a data set creates variable-length records and makes the observations shorter by removing duplicate data and patterns.

The advantages of compressing a file include reduced storage requirements and most importantly for performance, fewer I/O operations to read or write to the data. However, operations are more CPU-intensive because of the need to process each observation. Considering how much CPU performance has progressed compared to storage performance, such a trade-off is usually well worth it.

Because compression removes a record's empty or repeated data patterns, it works best on long records where there's a higher chance of data suitable for compression. If that's not the case, the compressed file can end up being larger than the uncompressed file. This provides an argument for not using compression indiscriminately.

A definitive answer on the wisdom of globally setting COMPRESS=Y at startup is difficult. However we note the following: a large majority of operations do benefit from compression, those that don't tend by nature to be small and quickly processed and finally SAS does have the capacity to automatically ignore counter-productive compression requests. As such, most users would from enabling compression globally at startup. As ever, each situation is different and one must chose according to their needs.

As a rule of thumb, a reduction in file size of less than 10 % makes the value of compression questionable, unless this freed space itself is of significant worth.

Two forms of compression are available to us: character compression (the default compression type) and binary compression, which is best suited for numbers. Binary compression is more CPU-intensive, but works better than character compression for records containing hundreds of bytes or more of numbers.

☞ If the data set will obviously not benefit from compression, SAS ignores the COMPRESS option and disables compression.

```
NOTE: Compression was disabled for data set ABC because compression overhead would
increase the size of the data set.
```

The decision SAS makes to ignore the COMPRESS option is taken conservatively and it is ultimately up to the user to make sure this kind of message doesn't appear, which signal that compressing had a detrimental effect by increasing both the size of the output data set size and the run time:

```
NOTE: Compressing data set ABC increased size by 100.00 percent.
```

Effectiveness of the COMPRESS option

The effectiveness of the SAS compression depends primarily upon 2 factors: observation length, and the nature of the data.

There is little point in discussing observation length here, except to say that the longer the observation the more likely SAS is to find repeated patterns that can be compressed effectively. Longer records will also more easily offset the compression overhead.

As for data, we could spend days looking at various examples, and perform benchmarks with your own data is the only way to find out exactly what the potential gains are. To get you started here are three examples demonstrating how data patterns affect compression efficiency.

Table 5.7: Compression effectiveness for some character values

Values	Char compression	Binary compression
Y,Y,Y,Y, etc (20 Ys)	Decreased size by 34.48 %	Decreased size by 28.21 %
Y,N,Y,N, etc (10 Ys, 10 Ns)	**Increased** size by 18.77 %	**Increased** size by 25.32 %

Even though 20 bytes are hard to compress, when *successive* variables have identical values, compression works well. In fact, 20 *successive* strings with length 1 and value 'Y' compress down to the same size as one string with length=20 and value 'YYYYYYYYYYYYYYYYYYYY' (this test is not shown).

Table 5.8: Compression effectiveness for some numeric values

Values	Char compression	Binary compression
0,0,0,0, etc (20 zeroes)	Decreased size by 88.80 %	Decreased size by 87.62 %
1,1,1,1, etc (20 ones)	Decreased size by 42.09 %	Decreased size by 62.16 %
1,2,3,4, etc	Decreased size by 49.48 %	Decreased size by 49.48 %
1,4,27,256,3125, etc	Decreased size by 15.68 %	**Increased** size by 6.81 %

The number zero compresses the best by far, and as expected the efficiency of compressing decreases as sequence complexity increases. Note that just changing the value from 0 to 1 lowers compression dramatically as can be seen in the first two examples.

Table 5.9: Compression effectiveness for numeric values with different lengths

Values	Char compression	Binary compression
1,1,1,1, etc (20 ones) Length=8	Decreased size by 42.09 %	Decreased size by 62.16 % 7884 pages instead of 20834
1,1,1,1, etc (20 ones) Length=3	**Increased** size by 8.79 %	**Increased** size by 12.05 % 9916 pages instead of 8850

In this case, reducing the variable length is less effective than compressing (8850 pages for uncompressed variables with length=3 and 7884 pages for compressed variables with length=8).

Still in this case, effecting both a length reduction and record compression is even worse and leads to increasing the record length.

The tests above were carried out running short DATA steps similar to this one:

```
data T(compress=char);
  array A[20] 8;
  do I=1 to 20;
   * A[I]=0;
   * A[I]=I**I;
   * A[I]=ifc(mod(I,2),'Y','N');
  end;
  do I=1 to 1e6;
    output;
  end;
run;
```

POINTOBS

SET AS DATA SET OPTION

If the ability to access compressed data by observation number is not needed, setting the option POINTOBS=NO improves performance by approximately 10% when creating or updating a compressed data set. Data retrieval performance is not impacted.

☞ The default value is POINTOBS=YES.

☞ There are very few cases where POINTOBS=NO is undesirable. The data set option OBS= is still usable with POINTOBS=NO.

☞ The POINT= option in the SET and MERGE statements is not usable with POINTOBS=NO and will generate an error:

```
ERROR: The POINT= data set option is not valid for the data set WORK.T, the data set must
be accessible by observation number for POINT= processing.
```

☞ The other feature that is disabled by using POINTOBS=NO is FSEDIT and FSVIEW's ability to go to an observation when typing the observation number as a command. If you try jump to an observation and option POINTOBS=NO has been used when creating the table, the following error will be generated:

```
ERROR: Access by observation number is not supported for this data set.
```

☞ If you don't need to use the option POINT= or the direct navigation options of SAS/FSP's older data viewers, you may want to set POINTOBS=NO in when creating large tables. Note that there is no global option to set this behaviour as default.

☞ POINTOBS=NO is effective only when creating a compressed data set. Otherwise it is ignored.

☞ The POINTOBS option is always set to NO when the REUSE option is set to YES. REUSE allows new observations to be written to space freed when other observations are updated or deleted in compressed data sets.

PROC OPTIONS

As we are nearing the end of this chapter, this last section is a reminder that PROC OPTIONS can display more information than most people realise. Here is an example of the information that is available from PROC OPTIONS:

```
proc options option=MEMSIZE value define; run;
```

This gives information about the current status of option MEMSIZE and about its usage.

```
      SAS (r) Proprietary Software Release 9.3   TS1M2

Option Value Information For SAS Option MEMSIZE
   Value: 3145728000
   Scope: SAS Session
   How option value set: SAS Session Startup Command Line

Option Definition Information for SAS Option MEMSIZE
   Group= MEMORY
   Group Description: Memory settings
   Group= PERFORMANCE
   Group Description: Performance settings
   Description: Specifies the limit on the total amount of memory to be used by the SAS
System
   Type: The option value is of type INTMAX
   Range of Values: The minimum is 0 and the maximum is 9223372036854775807
   Valid Syntax(any casing): MIN|MAX|n|nK|nM|nG|nT|hexadecimal
   Numeric Format: Usage of LOGNUMBERFORMAT does not impact the value format
   When Can Set: Session startup (command line or config) only
   Restricted: Your Site Administrator can restrict modification of this option
   Optsave: PROC Optsave or command Dmoptsave will not save this option
```

Who needs the online documentation when PROC OPTIONS gives so much detail?

Final words about options

Many more options affect the SAS system's performance, and we haven't covered the entirety of them here; just the ones that will have the most impact. Other performance options that are not covered include options those that govern the SQL optimiser. These can be seen by running:

```
proc options group=sql; run;
```

Further options that affect the performance of the SAS System can also be seen by running:

```
proc options group=performance; run;
```

Finally, you can see some options you never knew existed by running:

```
proc options internal; run;
```

Chapter 6

The Scalable Performance Data Engine

Introduction

Since many people still have never used SPDE, we'll start with a quick reminder, and then we'll test how its new features influence performance.

The SPDE Engine

Parallel processing can reduce the time it takes to process large amounts of data. With this in mind, SAS created the Scalable Performance Data Server. This piece of software runs on a dedicated server machine and executes requests coming from clients that connect to it. It stores its data in multiple partitions and splits the requests it receives into numerous threads. Each thread runs against a subset of the data, all threads run concurrently, and results can be returned faster. Scalability is the name of the game here: the goal is that by adding more hardware, you can make more, smaller, tasks and increase performance. Adding more CPUs and more I/O channels reduce the time it takes to run a query. This clever way to organise data and to access it allows SPDS to manage and process massive amounts of data very fast.

In their wisdom and generosity, SAS decided to include in Base SAS a little brother of SPDS's in the form of a new library engine. This engine does not provide all the power or flexibility of SPDS, but it still works on the same principle: split the files into partitions, split the processes into threads, and accelerate the creation of the results. The engine is called the Scalable Performance Data Engine (SPDE, also referred to as the speedy engine). It does not replace existing SAS engines; it is an addition to the tools already available in SAS. The scalability that SPDE offers can, when the circumstances are right, dramatically increase the processing speed for tasks such as processing WHERE clauses, creating indexes or appending data.

SPDS is optimised for large amounts of data, stored on machines that have access to numerous CPUs and can store their data on vast arrays of disks. Having these multiple resources allows SPDS to divide jobs into multiple chunks that run concurrently. SPDE is similar, and while it is not as powerful as a dedicated server environment, SPDE is intended for the rapid processing of very large data sets in machines that have similar characteristics: multiple CPUs and data stored in partitions across multiple disk volumes.

SPDE enables many features previously unavailable in Base SAS, including:

- support for gigabytes of data, removing the 2 GB limit some operating systems have
- CPU scalability on symmetric multiprocessor (SMP) machines
- parallel WHERE clause evaluation
- use of multiple indexes for WHERE clause evaluation
- implicit on-the-fly sorting on BY statements
- parallel data loading with PROC APPEND
- parallel data delivery to procedures
- parallel index creation
- better compression algorithms
- availability of bitmap indexing, whereas the Base SAS engines only use binary-tree indexing

SPDE runs on UNIX, Windows, z/OS (on HFS and ZFS file systems), and OpenVMS Alpha (on ODS-5 file systems).

How is SPDE organised?

SPDE data sets are physically different from Base SAS data sets.

The Base SAS engines store data in a single data set file that contains both the data and the metadata (the description of the data). The Base SAS engines also create another unique file for all the index information when one or several indexes are created.

In contrast, an SPDE data set is comprises at the very least 2 physical files. SPDE creates separate files for the data and for the data descriptor. If the SPDE data set is indexed, which it will most likely be, two index files are created for each index. Each of these four types of files is called an SPDE component file and each has a specific file extension.

So we can have four file types for each SPDE data set. All four types of SPDE component files can be made of one or more physical files that can span devices and directories, but is still referenced as one data set.

The four file types take these extension prefixes:

- MDF (MetaData File)
  This file contains the data set's metadata.
  The metadata includes information such as column names, sort order, index information, and the location of the other files in the data set. There is one MDF file per data set.
  These files are small.
- DPF (Data Partition File)
  This file contains the data proper. The data can be split across several DPF files. Each file is called a partition.
- HBX

This file is called the global index file and it contains a binary tree index, with de-duplicated list of all the values of the keys. If the keys are not unique then this file points to the IDX file for the repeated values.

There can be several HBX files per data set (one per index), but each index comprises a single HBX file unless the file had to be split due to lack of space.

- IDX

This file is called the segment index file and it contains a bitmap of the values that occur multiple times for a given index.

Each index comprises one IDX file, unless the file had to be split due to lack of space.

The SPDE file structure can be shown as follows:

Figure 6.1: An SPDE data set comprises several physical files

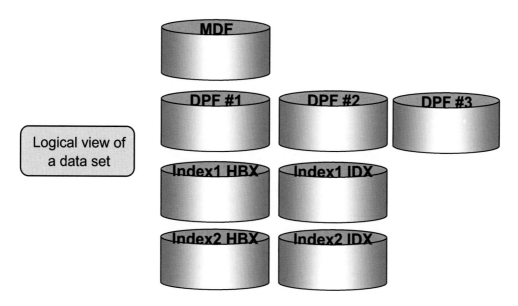

The strength of SPDE is that each file can be in a different location so more information can be accessed in parallel.

Here is the table SASHELP.CLASS in SPDE format, with 2 indexes. Only one partition file is created for this small table.

Figure 6.2: SASHELP.CLASS SPDE files

- class.dpf.03d9040a.0.1.spds9
- class.hbxage.03d9040a.0.1.spds9
- class.hbxsex.03d9040a.0.1.spds9
- class.idxage.03d9040a.0.1.spds9
- class.idxsex.03d9040a.0.1.spds9
- class.mdf.0.0.0.spds9

The data component differs from the metadata and index components in two ways:

- The partition size of the data component files can be controlled using the PARTSIZE= option. Obviously this is not possible for the other components' files and their size will solely depend on the information they contain.
- The location of the data component files is chosen by cycling through all the paths defined for DPF storage. In contrast, the metadata and index components are created in a single path until that path is full. Only then is the next path used. When an index component file fills the space available in the current file path, a new component file is created in the next path.

Table 6.1: Main differences between the Base SAS Engine and the SPD Engine.

	Feature	SPDE Engine	Base Engine
Positive	WHERE clause is optimized for parallel processing	Yes	No
	WHERE clause can use multiple indexes	Yes	No
	WHERE clause can use indexes with OR operator	Yes	No
	Creation of several indexes in parallel	Yes	No
	Parallel data loading with PROC APPEND	Yes	No
	Parallel index update with PROC APPEND	Yes	No
	Implicit sort on BY processing	Yes	No
	Data set compression (encryption impossible in SPDE)	Binary, Character Higher compression ratios	Binary, Character
Neutral	Number of files to store data	One file for the metadata, Data files can be partitioned	One file
	Number of files to store indexes	At least two files per index	One file
	Double Byte Character Support	Yes	Yes
	Largest number in the metadata's observation counter (the data set may have more)	$2^{63}-1$ (on all hosts)	$2^{31}-1$ (32-bit) $2^{63}-1$ (64-bit)
	Use OBS= & FIRSTOBS= system and data set options	Restrictions, use ENDOBS= & STARTOBS= instead	Yes
	Can be loaded in a hash table	Yes	Yes

Negative	Data set integrity constraints	No	Yes
	Data set audit trail	No	Yes
	Data set generations	No	Yes
	A data set can be loaded in memory with SASFILE	No	Yes
	A data set can be used as a source file in a view	No	Yes
	Library be RAM-based with MEMLIB option	No	Yes
	Library can store Views, Catalogs, MDDB files	No	Yes
	Cross-Environment Data Access (CEDA) support - to read data sets created on a different platform -	No	Yes
	Remote Library Services (RLS) support - to read remote data sets as local -	No	Yes
	Remote computing support	No/Yes [1]	Yes
	Remote data transfer support	No/Yes [1]	Yes
	SAS/SHARE support	No	Yes
	A data set can be encrypted	Yes, but not with compression	Yes
	Lowest locking record level	Member	Record
	Option DLCREATEDIR can be used - to create directory as the library is declared -	No	Yes
	Observations are returned in physical order	No if BY or WHERE used [2]	Yes
	DLDMGACTION= system and data set option	No [3]	Yes
	National Language Support	No	Yes
	SAS dictionary support	Partial [4]	Yes
	Move files to different locations	No in most cases [5]	Yes
	SAS Explorer refresh time	Slower. Every MDF file is read in full with each refresh.	Fast
	PROC DATASETS file lock	Wasteful [6]	Normal
	Some data sets are kept locked at random	Yes unless caching is disabled [7]	No
	SAS Functions and calls	No // WHERE processing for recent functions [8]	Yes
	File management always obvious	No [9]	Yes
	User-defined formats and informats	No // WHERE processing	Yes

[1] SAS/CONNECT is not supported with SPDE.

SAS technical support told me that when SAS Institute first developed SPDE, SAS/CONNECT didn't always interact well with the engine's threading model and would lock in some situations. A trap was put in place by the SAS/CONNECT developers "that specifically looks for use of SPDE and rejects the connection if found. That trap is still in place [in version 9.4]."
However, I have never had any issue using rsubmit or proc upload/download with SPDE data, so hopefully the restrictions in place will be lifted on these features.

[2] Setting option THREADNUM=1 retains the physical order of the observations.
   Setting option BYNOEQUALS=NO retains the physical order within each BY group.
   Using these options adversely impacts performance.

[3] Damage to partition data or metadata files is not detected and the files cannot be repaired.
   Damage to index files is detected and they can be repaired using PROC DATASETS's REPAIR statement.

[4] Some metadata, like filesize, is not handled properly by the dictionary.

[5] The file paths are stored as part of the metadata. The files cannot be moved by OS commands (unless all files are stored in the same location).

[6] PROC DATASETS opens every data set in the library, not just the data set being modified. There is no work-around for this behaviour. See *http://support.sas.com/kb/18/467.html*

[7] SPDE's file handle caching mechanism keeps some files locked and prevents user processes from accessing them. While this behaviour must provide some unspecified performance benefits, not being able access one's files makes this caching unusable on live data. In this case, the caching must be disabled. This can be done at invocation using option SPDEFILECACHE, or before defining SPDE libraries in the code. See *http://support.sas.com/kb/18/467.html*

[8] Functions introduced in SAS 9 like CAT() are not supported yet, and so using them kills performance.

[9] If one is not careful, some challenging situations can occur where identically named data files appear in the same location. In this example, two data files called TEST are stored in directory c:\tmp\d:

```
libname A spde 'c:\tmp' datapath=('c:\tmp\d'); data A.TEST;  run;
libname B spde                   'c:\tmp\d' ; data B.TEST;  run;
```

Furthermore, the messages written by SAS are not helpful when a data set's files have been deleted and some files are missing. Consider these examples where SAS doesn't find the files it expects and displays confusing messages in the log or leaves unused files behind. It is impossible to delete a corrupted data set, to read it, to repair it, or to recreate a new table.

```
* Metadata file missing ;
* * * * * * * * * * * * * * * * * * * * * * ;
libname SPEEDY spde 'c:\tmp';

* Create table;
data SPEEDY.TEST(compress=no
                partsize=32);
  do I=1 to 1e7; output; end; run;

* Delete the mdf file only;
x "del c:\tmp\test.mpf.* " ;

* Overwrite table
-> Succeeds but remnants from the
old table stay behind ;
data SPEEDY.TEST; X=1; run;
```

Name	Size
test.dpf.6ca17597.0.1.spds9	1 KB
test.mdf.0.0.0.spds9	35 KB
test.dpf.6ca17597.1.1.spds9	32,768 KB
test.dpf.6ca17597.2.1.spds9	32,768 KB
test.dpf.6ca17597.3.1.spds9	32,768 KB
test.dpf.6ca17597.4.1.spds9	25,178 KB

File remnants

```
* Data partition files missing ;
* * * * * * * * * * * * * * * * * * * * * * * * * ;

* Delete dpf file(s) only;
x "del c:\tmp\test.dpf.* " ;

* Delete table
-> Fails but no message in log;
proc delete data=SPEEDY.TEST; run;

* Delete table
-> NOTE: Table not found ;
proc datasets lib=SPEEDY;
  delete TEST; run;

* Repair table
-> ERROR: Table not found ;
proc datasets lib=SPEEDY;
  repair TEST; run;

* Read table
-> ERROR: Table not found;
data _null_; set SPEEDY.TEST; run;

* Overwrite table
-> ERROR: Table remnant found ;
data SPEEDY.TEST; X=1; run;
```

The benefits introduced by the SPDE engine are significant, but the numerous restrictions in place at the moment may mean that this solution is not suitable for all your data. Make sure to do a thorough assessment of the pros and cons.

✍ Please SAS Institute: Is it possible to integrate SPDE more tightly with SAS? The most useful features would probably be SAS/CONNECT support, view support, SASFILE statement support, metadata/dictionary integration, and helpful, comprehensive error messages when the SPDE files are not found as expected.

A closer look at SPDE's features

As we have seen, SPDE implements several features that can make data processing faster:

- It can partition data into different files. These files can be processed separately.
- It can use multiple CPUs to process different pieces of data concurrently. Some CPUs can be used to process data set partitions while others can process index files.
- It can create several indexes in parallel
- It uses more sophisticated indexing techniques.
- It compresses data much better than the V9 engine.
- It can spread files onto multiple I/O subsystems.
- It uses the language optimisation improvements described in table 6.1: on-the-fly BY processing, better WHERE clause optimization, parallel creation/update of indexes, parallel data loading.

Now that the presentation is done, let's look at the points in the list above.

Data split into partitions

The impact of spreading the data into several partitions will be studied while we look at other factors below.

Concurrent work with multiple CPUs

SPDE's ability to use multiple CPUs at the same timer to process data can drastically accelerate processes. We'll look at two examples using DATA steps. Data steps aren't multi-threaded when using the V9 engine, but can be when accessing data using the SPDE engine if the THREADNUM option is used.

☞ Note that the CPUCOUNT option has no effect on the SPDE engine. Use THREADNUM.

For the test, we create a data set, and we read of subset of it while varying the number of threads available. So that's three tests:

- SPDE engine with 1 thread
- SPDE engine with 4 threads
- V9 Engine

In order to check whether more threads take advantage of more data partitions and how they influence index usage, we test 3 cases:

- SPDE engine with the data set split into 2 partitions and no index,
- SPDE engine with the data set split into 8 partitions and no index,
- SPDE engine with the data set split into 2 partitions and an index.

We want to focus on the performance of the SPDE data structures here, and compare to it to the performance offered by the Base engine. While SPDE was designed for spreading data loads across many I/O subsystems, testing using such a configuration would not allow for a meaningful

136

comparison between the two engines. Furthermore, distributed storage can exist in an infinity of forms, and any one setup would not be representative of yours.

For these reasons, the tests will run on a single SSD. This will allow to truly assess the benefits of this new engine compared to the V9 engine, without taking into account the further benefits offered by deploying multiple data storage points.

The tests use variations on this code:

```
************** WRITE DATA ****************;
libname SPEEDY spde "%sysfunc(pathname(work))";
data SPEEDY. /* or WORK library*/ TEST
             (partsize = 20M /* or 100M        */
              index    = (I) /* or no index   */
              threadnum= 1   /* or 4 threads */);
  do I=1 to 2e7;
    output;
  end;
run;

************** READ DATA ****************;
data _null_;
  set SPEEDY.        /* or WORK library*/ TEST
    (threadnum = 1 /* or 4 threads    */
     Where     = ( 2e5 < I < 3e5 ));
run;
```

Let's start by the read times. Here are 2 charts showing the run times of the second DATA step.

Figure 6.3: Influence of the number of CPUs when reading SPDE data

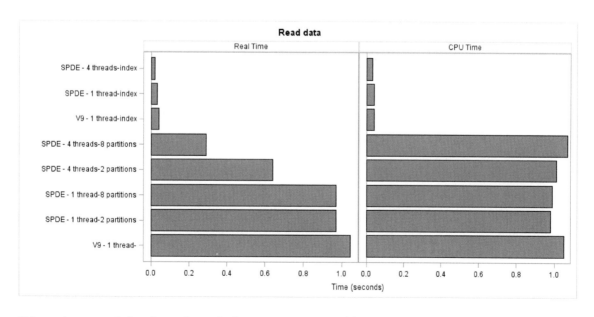

It is easier to read the charts from the bottom up, as speed increases.

The following patterns are obvious:

- The V9 engine always takes longer to complete the different tasks than the SPDE engine.
- Adding partitions and no extra threads brings little benefit
- Adding more partitions and more threads dramatically shrinks the run time. This comes at the expense of a slightly higher CPU load as managing all the threads brings some overhead.

SPDE looks very good here. Is there anything not to like in this example?

Possibly:

Figure 6.4: Influence of the number of CPUs when creating SPDE data

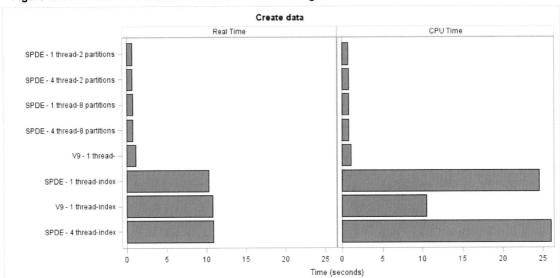

When creating a data set, SPDE is faster than the V9 engine is most cases. Two things to note however:

- More partitions and more threads slow down (slightly) this table creation process.
- When creating an index, SDPE's CPU consumption increases dramatically while the real time is similar to the Base engine's. We will look at this in the next section.

Simultaneous indexing

SPDE allows the concomitant creation of several indexes. As usual, this comes at the cost of a higher CPU usage. Here, as an example, we create 3 indexes on a 230 MB data set while varying three parameters: the number of threads, the number of data set partitions and whether the ASYNCINDEX option that allows concurrent index creation is enabled.

Code:

```
%macro loop;
%do asyncindexN=1 %to 2;
 %let asyncindex=%sysfunc(choosec(&asyncindexN,no,yes));
 %do partsize=20 %to 100 %by 40;
  %do threadnum=1 %to 8;
   %put asyncindex=&asyncindex partsize=&partsize threadnum=&threadnum;
   data SPEEDY.TEST(partsize  = &partsize.M
                    threadnum = &threadnum.
                    asyncindex= &asyncindex.
                    index     = (I J K) );
     do I=1 to 1e7;
       J=I; K=I; output;
     end;
   run;
  %end;
 %end;
%end;
%mend;
%loop
```

Figure 6.5: SPDE parallel indexing – Real time

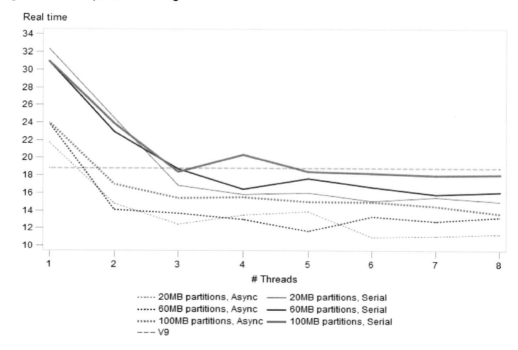

The horizontal dashed line shows the time the V9 engine takes to create the indexes.

Observations:

- As we saw earlier, SPDE takes a lot longer than the V9 engine if only one thread is used. Using asynchronous (i.e. simultaneous) index creation helps.
- If several threads are used but concurrent index creation is not enabled, SPDE can beats the V9 reference time (solid lines).
- Parallel index creation works really well: as soon as we have 2 threads, the V9 time is easily bettered (dotted lines).
- Having smaller, more numerous partitions brings significant gains in all cases.

Figure 6.6: SPDE parallel indexing – CPU time

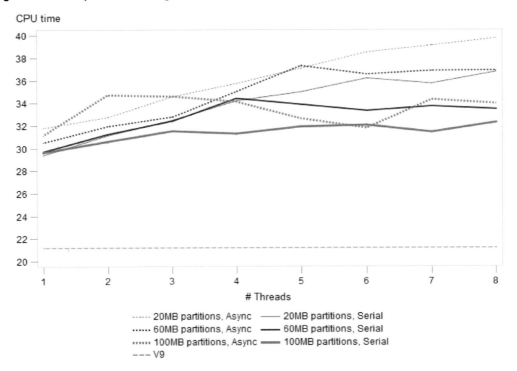

We can see here how CPU-hungry SPDE is when creating indexes. It uses 50% to 100% more CPU than the V9 engine does. Matching the real time gains, smaller data set partitions and parallel threading need more CPU power: the more time is saved, the more CPU is consumed.

Parallel index creation works well in SPDE to save time, but at the cost of a much higher CPU consumption.

Better indexing techniques

Several improvements have been made to the indexes used by the V9 engine.

Hybrid index

SPDE implements a new indexing technique that is a combination of a binary tree (also called B-tree) and a bitmap. If a variable's value in the data set is unique, the location of that observation is stored in the B-tree index. If the value occurs in multiple observations in the data set, there is one entry in the B-tree and a pointer to a bitmap holding the locations of the relevant observations. The base SAS engine in contrast only support B-trees.

The WHERE clause is adapted to parallel processing

When a query contains a where clause and when the SPDE engine creates multiple threads, it applies the where clause to each of the threads.

The WHERE clauses can use multiple indexes

While the V9 engine chooses one index to accelerate the processing of WHERE clause, the SPDE engine can use several indexes.

The WHERE clauses can use indexes which contain the OR operator

While the V9 engine choose one index to accelerate the processing of WHERE clause, the SPDE engine can use several indexes.

Let's see how this translates in the real world. We create a 100-million row table with 2 indexes (cardinality 1e8 and 1e4) and see how fast data can be retrieved using three different where clauses:

- Test 1: A where clause on one indexed variable
- Test 2: A where clause on two indexed variables using the AND operator
- Test 3: A where clause on two indexed variables using the OR operator

Figure 6.7: SPDE index retrieval efficiency – Real time

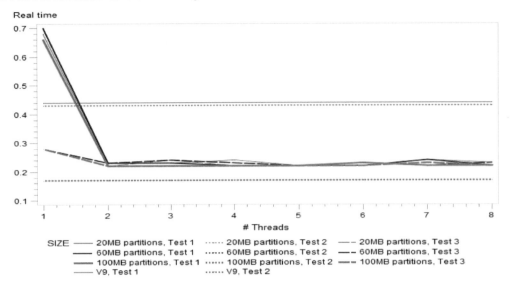

Note that the V9+Test 3 plot is missing from the graph above as it took 8 seconds to complete: the V9 engine doesn't use indexes with OR clauses present and must scan the whole data set.

The only case where SPDE is slower than V9 is when only one index is needed *and* only one thread is used. In all other cases, SPDE is much faster as V9.

Figure 6.8: SPDE index retrieval speed – CPU time

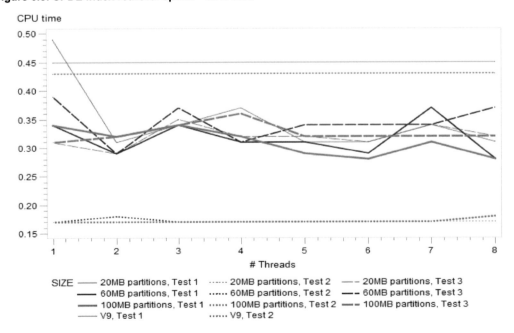

Not only is SPDE faster than V9 for indexed data retrieval, it also uses fewer resources. The investment in extra CPU time when creating the index pays off.

We used two simple indexes for the previous test. The result differs somewhat if we use a composite index instead. Here are the plots for tests 1 and 2.

Figure 6.9: SPDE composite index retrieval speed, no OR operator – Real time

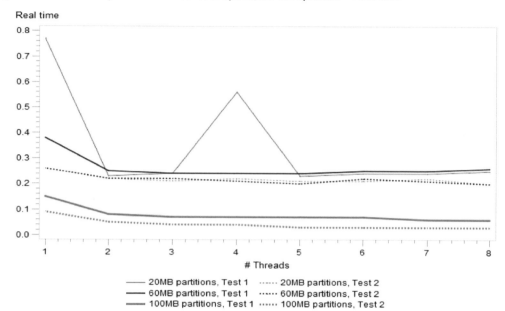

Figure 6.10: SPDE composite index retrieval speed, no OR operator – CPU time

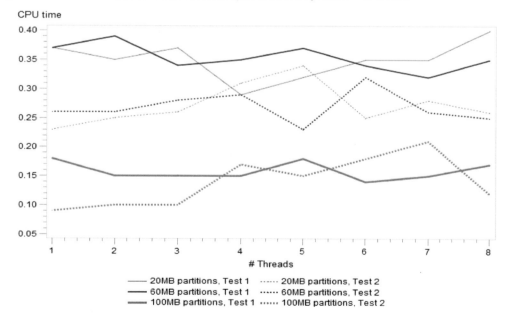

Using a composite index does not dramatically change SPDE's behaviour for these two tests. Larger partitions might help boost the speed in this case.

Test 3 (the OR clause) and the V9 results are plotted separately as they took much longer.

Figure 6.11: SPDE composite index retrieval speed, with OR operator – Real time

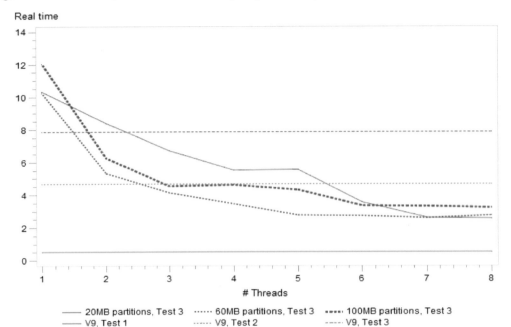

Figure 6.12: SPDE composite index retrieval speed, with OR operator – CPU time

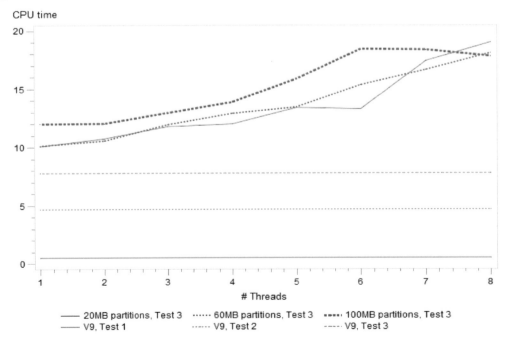

In light of the fact that SPDE can use single indexes concurrently, and considering how performance degrades when the OR operator is used on composite indexes, one should test carefully before choosing to implement composite indexes rather than simple indexes with SPDE.

Compression

To see how compression ratios are improved with SPDE, we'll use similar data patterns to that used when discussing the compress option.

Table 6.2: Values used for compression tests

Test Number	Values	# Variables	Variable Length
1	0,0,0,0, etc	20	8
2	1,1,1,1, etc	20	8
3	1,2,3,4, etc	20	8
4	1,4,27,256,3125, etc	20	8
5	Y,Y,Y,Y, etc (20 Ys)	20	1
6	Y,N,Y,N, etc (10 Ys, 10 Ns)	20	1
7	1,1,1,1, etc	20	3
8	1 then 2 then 3 then 4 etc	1	8

Note that for test 8, SAS chose to disable compression when using the V9 engine because compression overhead would have increased the size of the data set.

Here are the results for these 8 data patterns, first when using binary compression and then using character compression.

Figure 6.13: SPDE Binary compression

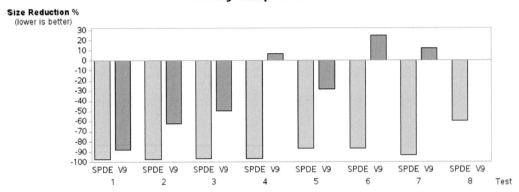

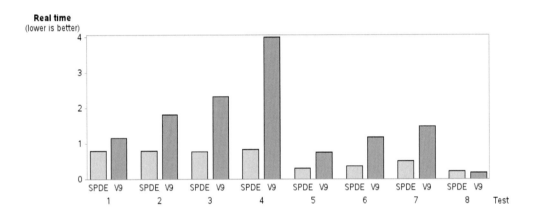

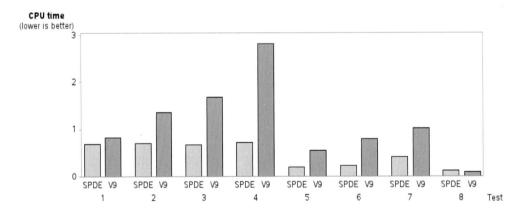

Wow! These graphs show the power of SPDE's binary compression routines. Every pattern compresses well, even character values and single variable tables. On top of this, real times and CPU times are significantly lower than what the V9 engine consumes. The worst happens for test 4, where the V9 engine tries hard to compress the data, uses a large amount of CPU (and elapse) time, and finally ends up increasing the size of the dataset.

This compression capability is a momentous step forward. For this reason alone, SPDE seriously deserves your consideration.

Figure 6.14: SPDE Character compression

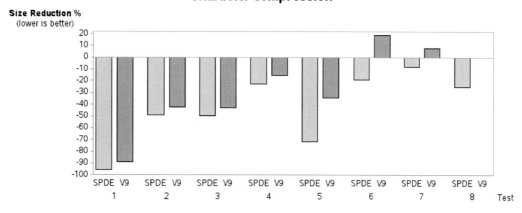

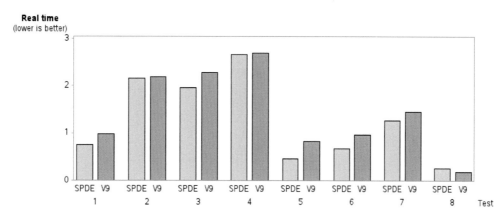

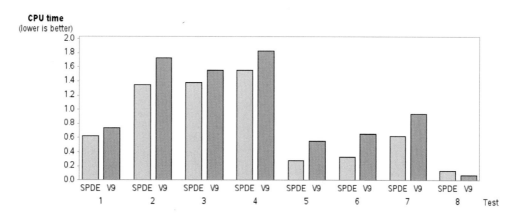

Character compression still shows SPDE outclassing the V9 engine in pretty much every measure and every case, but not as convincingly as with binary compression. Binary compression compresses our sample character data better than character compression.

Enabling binary compression by default looks like a no-brainer, even if as usual, specific datasets may need a different treatment.

On-the-fly implicit sorting

One of the innovative features of SDPE's is the ability to use a table in sorted order even if the table is not sorted or indexed. While this feature is not revolutionary, it can be nice to avoid writing a sorting step before using data, so why not? Let's look at this feature.

We compare an implicit sort, an explicit sort and an index using both the SPDE and V9 engines.

```
options compress=no msglevel=I nofullstimer;
libname SPEEDY spde "%sysfunc(pathname(WORK))";
%macro test(lib);                      %* Test routine;
  data _null_; set &lib..TEST; by I; run;
%mend;

data SPEEDY.TEST WORK.TEST;        %* Create test data sorted by desc I;
  length X $1016;
  do I=1e6 to 1 by -1;
    output;
  end;
run;

%test(SPEEDY);                     %* SPDE - On-the-fly Sort;

proc sort data=SPEEDY.TEST
          out= SPEEDY.TEST1;
  by I;
%test(SPEEDY);                     %* SPDE - Explicit Sort;

proc sql;
  create index I on SPEEDY.TEST;
%test(SPEEDY);                     %* SPDE - Index;

proc sql;                                    ;
  create view _V  as select * from TEST order by I;
%test(WORK);                       %* Base - On-the-fly Sort

proc sort data=TEST out=TEST1;
  by I;
%test(WORK);                       %* Base - Explicit Sort;

proc sql;
  create index I on WORK.TEST;
%test(WORK);                       %* Base - Index;
```

Table 6.3: Results of BY processing for the SPDE engine

SPDE Test	Real Time (seconds)	CPU Time (seconds)
Implicit sort	4.1 (4.05 data step)	5.0 (4.99 data step)
Explicit sort	8.1 (6.86 sort + 1.20 data)	7.7 (6.08 sort + 1.63 data)
Index	2.2 (0.78 sql + 1.40 data)	2.9 (1.28 sql + 1.63 data)

I must admit that I was a bit cynical when I first heard of SPDE's implicit sort capability. I was wrong however: it works well.

For a one-off sort on data that won't be reused, it is generally faster to rely on SPDE's implicit sorting ability than to explicitly sort a table.

Less coding, more speed: All good.

This is not always the best solution however, and in the case of our test data, building an index is by far the fastest way to achieve our goal.

A part of the savings is probably due to not writing an output file to disk. We can we try to do the same with the base engine and create a view.

Table 6.4: Results of BY processing for the V9 engine

V9 Test	Real Time (seconds)	CPU Time (seconds)
Implicit sort	5.6 (0.04 sql + 5.58[1] data)	7.0 (0.00 sql + 6.98 data)
Explicit sort	4.4 (3.54 sort + 0.78 data)	4.7 (3.96 sort + 0.78 data)
Index	2.4 (0.96 sql + 1.41 data)	2.6 (1.21 sql + 1.41 data)

[1] This time is very erratic and often jumps to over a minute

Using the V9 engine, on-the-fly sorting is slower than with the SPDE engine, which is not really surprising as views incur non-negligible overheads.

Using our data, the V9 explicit sort runs faster than both V9's implicit on-the-fly sort and SPDE's explicit sort. The V9 engine also has an edge for the index test. So SPDE is not a silver bullet here, but its implicit sort does offer a speed boost.

As usual, your mileage may vary and so on, but make sure to consider the implicit sort feature of SPDE's. It can beat a hard PROC SORT.

Multiple paths

A defining characteristic of the SPDE engine is its physical file layout, where the data is partitioned into separate files which can be spread onto separate IO subsystems. This in turn allows two things: each partition can be processed by its own thread, and each partition is served by its own disk.

However, RAID arrays also allow spreading files across multiple disks. So does SPDE's data partition distribution bring any advantages over just letting a RAID drive do the job of spreading the I/Os? Let's have a look.

For this test, I'll describe the testing platform in more details. The other tests were very dependent on the hardware used, but this one even more so. I used a Windows 64 PC with 2 CPUs and 5 disks: One system hard drive and four data SSDs (Intel 320 160GB and 600GB, 2 x Samsung EVO840 120GB).

The metadata will go to the system drive C:, and the data will be spread in different manners for each one of seven tests:

- One data path
- Two data paths pointing to two disks
- Three data paths pointing to three disks
- Four data paths pointing to four disks
- One data path pointing to a 2-disk RAID stripe
- One data path pointing to a 3-disk RAID stripe
- One data path pointing to a 4-disk RAID stripe

This can be seen in the definition of the libraries:

```
libname ONEDRV    spde 'c:\test'  datapath=('d:\test' );
libname TWODRV    spde 'c:\test'  datapath=('d:\test' 'i:\test' );
libname THREEDRV  spde 'c:\test'  datapath=('d:\test' 'i:\test'
                                            'g:\test' );
libname FOURDRV   spde 'c:\test'  datapath=('d:\test' 'i:\test'
                                            'g:\test' 'j:\test' );
libname RAID0_2   spde 'c:\test'  datapath=('k:\test' );
libname RAID0_3   spde 'c:\test'  datapath=('l:\test' );
libname RAID0_4   spde 'c:\test'  datapath=('m:\test' );
```

Now, the test will consist on a pure-write DATA step whereby we create a 5GB table, followed by a pure-read test, and lastly a test where reads and writes take place simultaneously. These three tests are run five times. The data set partitions are the default 128 MB in size.

Figure 6.15: Results of the RAID vs SPDE data distribution speed test

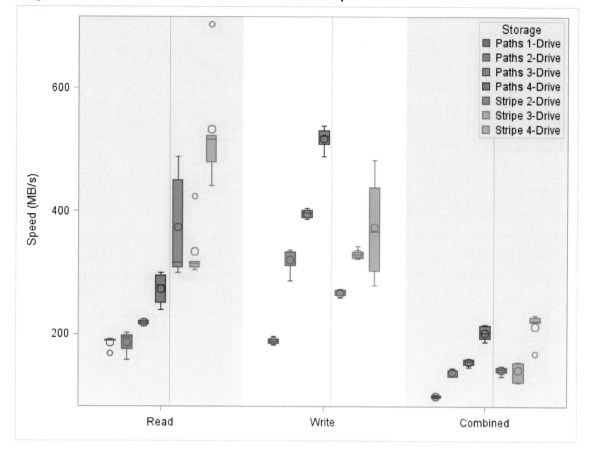

For each test, the bars are drawn left to right in the legend order.

When reading, SPDE improves slightly its performance when 3 or 4 disks are available in its library path. SPDE's leverage of concatenated-paths libraries is not very convincing though, especially when compared with the huge speed improvements brought by using a RAID array on the same drives.

When writing, the RAID speeds are comparable to their read speed, if a bit lower. SPDE on the other hand is very happy to use the several paths available to it and easily exceeds the RAID speeds.

For the combined read & write operation, the overall speeds are of course much lower. No significant difference can be seen between the solutions that span drives using a RAID array and those that span drives using a concatenated library. This is probably because the lower read and higher write speeds of the SPDE libraries cancel out each other to match the more consistent level of the RAID storage's speeds.

So does SPDE's ability to distribute its data bring any benefits? Unfortunately, we can't assume so from this small test. If your tables are mostly used in read mode, as most data warehouses are, it would definitely pay to do a benchmark before committing to either solution. SPDE's write speeds are a lot more convincing, but are not as useful.

Another aspect to consider is the geographic and management constraints of the two ways to organise disk space. If the drives are physically scattered, RAID may not be an option. On the other hand, if RAID is an option, it presents the advantage of ease of management: one spacious logical path where all the files are, rather than a collection of paths. Having one fast storage location also presents the advantage that access to other files, such as indexes, metadata files or regular datasets can easily be accelerated as well.

☞ The tests use a RAID0 configuration. Permanent data would of course never be stored in such an unreliable array. This however does not affect the results of the benchmark above, which only aims to compare identical storage systems used in various ways.

Conclusion

There is no doubt that the SPDE engine brings important performance –and other– benefits. If you haven't done so already, familiarise yourself with this (not so) new comer, its remarkable qualities and its numerous limitations as of version 9.4, and then test to decide which of your data and processes can leverage this new engine.

Chapter 7

Joining Tables

Introduction

There are countless sources of information about what views and hash tables are and how to use them, what the different SQL operators do, or how indexes work. I will assume that these topics are familiar to the reader and once again, I will focus on the performance side of using these various tools in different situations.

This chapter will never be complete. There exists an infinite number of ways to join tables, and each case is different. Tables can be joined vertically (concatenation) or horizontally, or both. The join can be between two tables or between many more, or even a table against itself. Some tables in the join will be large and some small, some tables will be narrow (few columns, many rows) and some wide (few rows). Each join can be an intersection or a left join (all rows from a table) or a union (all rows from contributing tables) or other less common join types. The goal may be to add many columns or simply to validate a few values. The number of matches may be a few rows or millions of rows. Input tables may be sorted or indexed or without any order. Output tables may need to be sorted or not. The data combinations are endless.

Furthermore, SAS has many syntaxes to read and write tables. Data steps use the SET, MERGE, UPDATE and MODIFY statements, together with their options like KEY= or POINT=. Data steps can also use hash tables. SAS can also use the CREATE, UPDATE, INSERT and DELETE statement in PROC SQL, together with SQL operators join, union, intersect and except and all their many variants, as well as the exists and other nested subquery operators. The SAS language offers a huge array of methods to join data. Even formats or macro variables can be used.

The variations are infinite, each join is unique, and each must be looked at on its own merit. This means that you will find no silver bullet in this chapter for joining tables. What you will find are explanations and examples to help you consider the parameters involved in making fast joins.

As with all data processing, the main goal when joining tables is to reduce the number of I/O operations, and to generate sequential I/O operations. Keep this is mind while reading this chapter, and the considerations exposed should become obvious.

General considerations

There are basically two ways to merge tables:

The simplest way is to sort the tables. They can then be read sequentially, and each time key values (or row number) match, the observations are joined. The initial sort is expensive, but the subsequent process is highly efficient.

The second way is to read one table (usually sequentially), and fetch the matching observations from other table(s) for each key value(s) in the first table. All observations except possibly those from the first table are typically read in a random fashion.

This technique avoids sorting, but is slower and becomes costly if the number of observations to fetch is high. At some point, it often becomes cheaper to sort the tables than to perform a large number of random accesses.

There are ways to improve the speed of the random reads. One method is to create indexes. Another method is to load the table(s) in memory, typically as hash table(s). Loading a table in memory performs a sequential disk read, and all the subsequent random reads are made from very fast RAM.

Simple comparison of 9 techniques

Before delving into more details, let's have a first look at these various methods.

Here is the test data: 10 million rows, 2 columns.

```data TAB1 TAB2(rename=(I=J)); do I=1 to 1e7; KEY=int(ranuni(0)*1e15); output; end; run;```	We create two tables with 10 million rows and 2 columns. The tests will retrieve variable J from the second table TAB2 and add it to the first table TAB1.

Example 1: Sort both tables (this yields a sorted output)

```proc sort data=TAB1 out=SORTED1; * 5s; by KEY; proc sort data=TAB2 out=SORTED2; * 5s; by KEY; data _null_; * 2s; merge SORTED1 SORTED2; by KEY; run;```	The sorts are a bit expensive, but the two tables can then be joined really fast, and the output is sorted. Real Time= 5 + 5 + 2 = 12 seconds

```data _null_; * 1s; merge SORTED1 SORTED2; run;```	I am also showing here an atypical merge, without key. This is an option allowed by the merge statement, and it cuts the processing time in half. A BY statement is sometimes not necessary, in which case it should be omitted.

Example 2: Hash table (the output is not sorted)

```data _null_; * 30s; set TAB1; if _N_=1 then do; dcl hash TAB2(dataset:'TAB2'); TAB2.definekey('KEY'); TAB2.definedata('J'); TAB2.definedone(); K=.; end; RC=TAB2.find(); run;```	In this case, because sorting is fast (due to the small size of the table and to its narrowness), using a hash table takes longer than sorting. Real Time= 30 seconds

Example 3: Index on one table (the output is not sorted)

```proc sql; * 5/10 s; create index KEY on TAB2(KEY); quit; data _null_; * 4:10/60 s; set TAB1; set TAB2 key= KEY ; run;```	Using an index is much slower because the lookup table is accessed randomly. This method is better used when a small number of records are accessed. Real Time = 265 seconds *Note: the second time is the CPU time.*

Example 4: Index on both tables (the output is sorted)

```proc sql; * 5/10 s; create index KEY on TAB1(KEY); quit; data _null_; * 20:17/4:25.32 ; set TAB1 TAB2; by KEY; if _N_ > 1e5 then stop; run;```	This is slower still as we access both tables randomly via an index. Real Time = 1200 seconds. *Don't do this.*

155

Example 5: Index on both tables in memory (the output is sorted)

| ```
sasfile TAB1 open;
sasfile TAB2 open;
data _null_;      * 26/22 s;
  set TAB1 TAB2;
  by KEY;
run;
sasfile TAB1 close;
sasfile TAB2 close;
``` | One way to accelerate the use of indexes it to make random access calls into memory. This is only possible if enough RAM is available.<br><br>Consider the huge improvement:<br><br>Real Time = 36 seconds (10 s for building the indexes and 26 s joining) |

Example 6: Index on one table in memory (the output is not sorted)

| ```
sasfile TAB2 open;
data _null_;      * 43/42 s;
  set TAB1;
  set TAB2 key= KEY ;
run;
sasfile TAB2 close;
``` | Even though we only access one table randomly here, the overhead of the KEY= option is so high that this method is about twice as slow as the previous join.<br><br>Using a BY statement (as in Example 5) lets SAS manage the key-matching process. Using KEY= allows the user to manage the key, but at a huge cost. |

What we have seen about data step joins is also true when joining with PROC SQL.

Example 7: Join unsorted tables with PROC SQL

| ```
proc sql _method;
  select max(I), max(J)
  from TAB1, TAB2
  where TAB1.KEY = TAB2.KEY;
quit;

 sqxslct
    sqxsumn
       sqxjm
          sqxsort
             sqxsrc( WORK.TAB1 )
          sqxsort
             sqxsrc( WORK.TAB2 )

 real time          12.89 seconds
 user cpu time      18.42 seconds
 system cpu time    0.96 seconds
 memory             397354.75k
 OS Memory          418452.00k
``` | The result here is similar to Example 1.<br><br><br>We can see that the tables were sorted then joined.<br><br><br><br>The resources used are comparable to those of the data step in Example 1. |
```

Example 8: Join unsorted tables with proc SQL, with less data

``
proc sql _method;
   select max(I)
   from TAB1, TAB2
   where TAB1.KEY =TAB2.KEY;
quit;
 	
   sqxslct
      sqxsumn
         sqxjhsh
            sqxsrc(WORK.TAB1)
            sqxsrc(WORK.TAB2)
 	
   real time   10.53 seconds
   user cpu time   10.31 seconds
   system cpu time   0.20 seconds
   memory   439672.50k
   OS Memory   461648.00k
``
	Because we requested less data (no need to consider variable J), PROC SQL decided that the data can fit in memory in a hash table.
	
	The elapse time is the best so far.
	
	Similarly to when using for KEY= to manage index use (as in Example 6 vs 5), allowing the user to manage the hash table (Example 2) brings a large overhead that proc SQL does not have to support here.

Example 9: Join sorted tables with proc SQL

``
proc sql _method;
   select max(I)
   from SORTED1, SORTED2
   where SORTED1.KEY =SORTED2.KEY;
quit;
 	
   sqxcrta
      sqxjm
         sqxsrc(WORK.SORTED1)
         sqxsrc(WORK.SORTED2)
 	
      real time   4.40 seconds
      user cpu time   4.15 seconds
      system cpu time   0.23 seconds
      memory   3643.09k
      OS Memory   26464.00k
``
	Proc SQL knows that the tables are sorted, so it simply reads them sequentially.
	
	This is identical to the last step of Example 1.
	
	A data step is much more efficient for this sequential-read match.

We have seen that indexes are slow if a large proportion of the table is retrieved, and that sorting may be faster.

Each join has a breakeven point where sorting becomes faster if more than a certain proportion of the observations are retrieved. Let's look at the breakeven point for our two tables.

Case Studies

Break-even point for various joins

For this test, we keep the same tables, with either both tables being sorted before the match, or TAB2 being indexed. We then retrieve a growing portion from table TAB2.

```
%* Both tables sorted;
proc sort data=TAB1 out=SORTED1; by KEY; run;
proc sort data=TAB2 out=SORTED2; by KEY; run;  * 10/15s ;

data _null_; merge SORTED1 SORTED2(obs=   10000); by KEY; run; * 1.2 s;
data _null_; merge SORTED1 SORTED2(obs=  100000); by KEY; run; * 1.2 s;
data _null_; merge SORTED1 SORTED2(obs= 1000000); by KEY; run; * 1.3 s;
data _null_; merge SORTED1 SORTED2(obs=10000000); by KEY; run; * 2.6 s;


%* Lookup table indexed;                               *Real/CPU ;
proc sql; create index J on TAB2(KEY); quit;           *  5/8 s;

data _null_; set TAB1; if _N_<1e4 then set TAB2 key=KEY; run; *  1/1 s;
data _null_; set TAB1; if _N_<1e5 then set TAB2 key=KEY; run; *  3/1 s;
data _null_; set TAB1; if _N_<3e5 then set TAB2 key=KEY; run; *  6/2 s;
data _null_; set TAB1; if _N_<1e6 then set TAB2 key=KEY; run; * 20/6 s;
```

Figure 7.1: Break-even point for an all-column joins, by percentage of rows retrieved

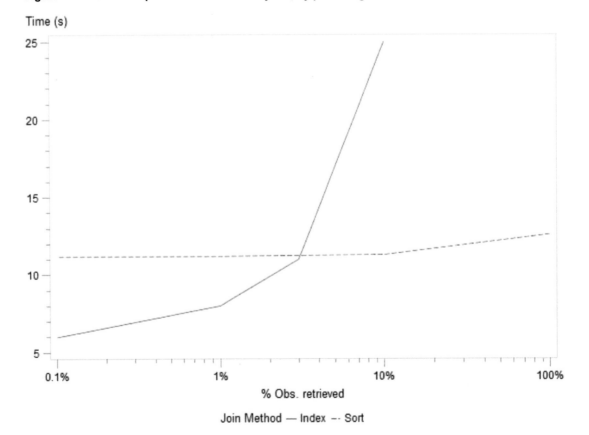

For our data, the breakeven point is at about 3% of the data retrieved. If retrieving more data, it becomes cheaper to sort. A rule of thumb is that indexes generally become too costly when retrieving more than 5 to 15% of the data.

For a given number a rows, the wider the table and the costlier the sort, whereas the cost of indexing will increase much more slowly. We can see this by using the same data, and retrieving a constant 5% of the rows while adding more and more columns.

```
%macro merges(nbvars);

  data TAB1 TAB2(rename=(I=J));
    length A1-A&nbvars. 8;
    do I=1 to 1e7; KEY=int(ranuni(0)*1e15); output; end;
  run;

  proc sort data=TAB1 out=SORTED1;
    by KEY;
  run;

  proc sort data=TAB2 out=SORTED2;
    by KEY;
  run;

  data _null_;
    merge SORTED1 SORTED2(obs=500000);
    by KEY;
  run;

  proc sql;
    create index KEY on TAB2(KEY);
  quit;

  data _null_;
    set TAB1;
    if _N_<5e5 then set TAB2 key= KEY;
  run;

%mend;         %*Real sort+merge   index+fetch;

%merges(1);   %*  sort:10+1.5 - index:5+11 ;
%merges(5);   %*  sort:14+2   - index:6+11 ;
%merges(10);  %*  sort:17+4   - index:6+11 ;
%merges(15);  %*  sort:20+7   - index:6+11 ;
%merges(20);  %*  sort:26+8   - index:6+11 ;
```

Figure 7.2: Break-even point for 5% of the rows retrieved depending on the width of the tables

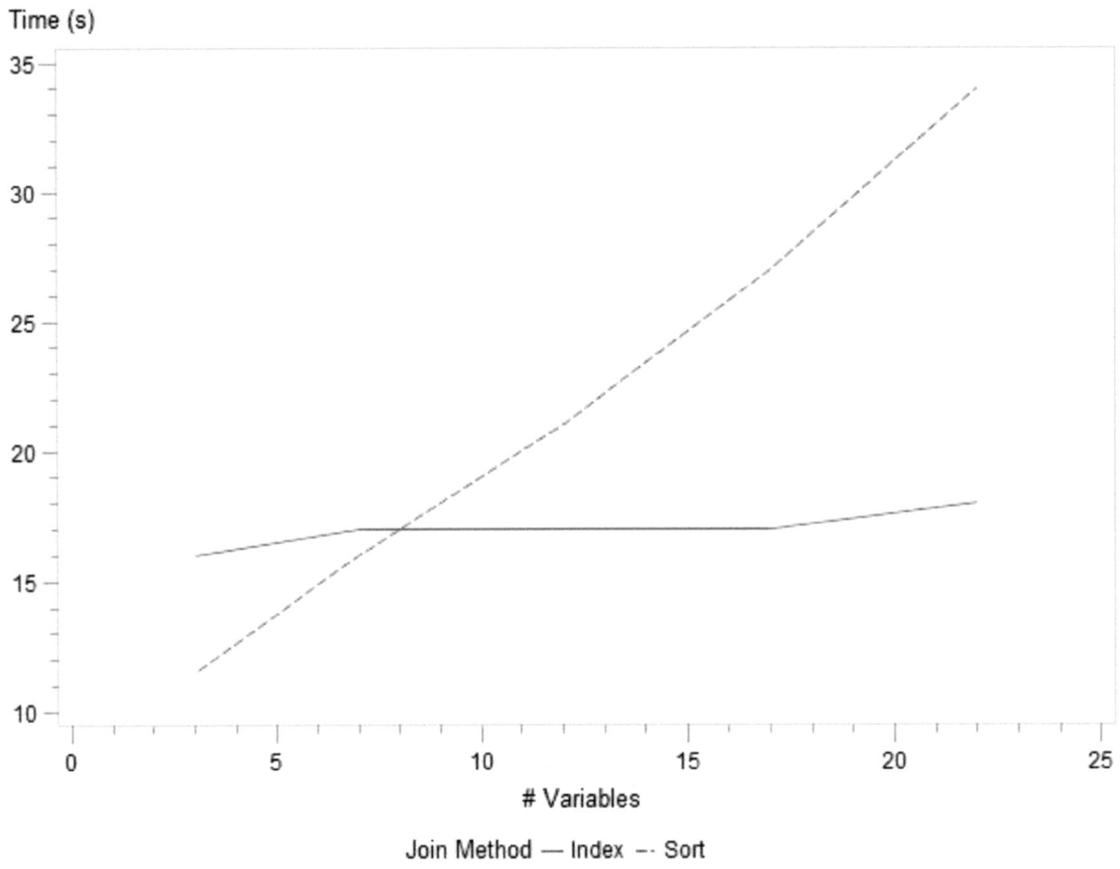

As the number of variables increases, the cost of the sort also increases, while the cost of indexing and retrieval is not nearly as impacted.

Note that the slope of the slanted curve is dramatically different between the two graphs. This becomes even more obvious if plotting the first graph on a linear scale.

Figure 7.3: Break-even point by percentage of rows retrieved (using a linear scale)

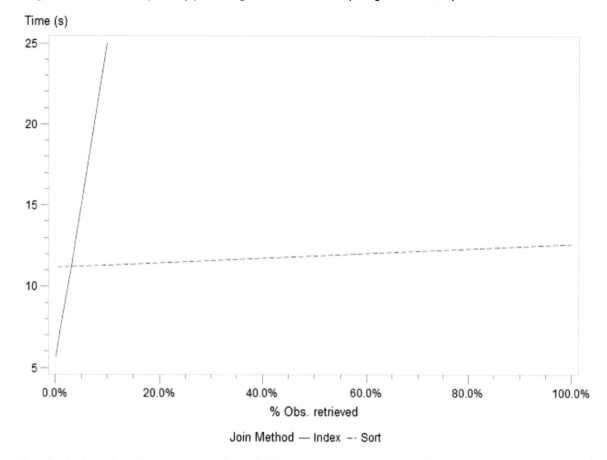

The clock time deteriorates extremely quickly as more matches are added when using the index. So in case of doubt or when there is no obvious advantage to either method for your data in your environment, it is often better to stray on the side of sorting: misidentifying the best method is less likely to bring the process to its knees.

The examples above should have given you a good overview of the strong (and weak) points of different join methods. Let's now continue by looking at more specific scenarios.

What is the fastest merge method depending on the shape of the join?

We'll now benchmark a typical two-table join scenario and deepen our knowledge of the join methods' strong and weak points: we'll gradually increase the number of rows and the number of columns retrieved from the second table. We start with two 10-million-row 50-column unsorted tables, and from 1% to 100% of the rows and from 1 to 50 columns from the second "look-up" table. The results given are the real times, in seconds.

When the method yields the worst time of all methods, the figures are written is smaller size.

When the method yields the best time of all methods, the figures are shaded.

Note: The methods used are: Sort + Merge by, Index + Set Key=, Sasfile + Index + Set Key=, and hash table. Only the first method yields a sorted output; if you need to merge again later on, this is a clear advantage. Using formats was never a contender as creating a format with millions of values takes several minutes.

Table 7.1: Elapse times for join method Sort + Merge By

# Columns Retrieved	% of Rows Retrieved					
	1%	5%	10%	20%	50%	100%
1	79	80	81	84	79	78
5	81	79	79	79	79	79
10	89	88	89	95	93	90
20	93	94	92	95	90	90
30	95	95	95	96	95	94
40	99	98	102	99	100	99
50	104	105	105	105	105	110

Table 7.2: Elapse times with for method Hash table

# Columns Retrieved	% of Rows Retrieved					
	1%	5%	10%	20%	50%	100%
1	57	59	58	60	65	73
5	56	57	59	61	66	77
10	61	63	64	69	69	80
20	66	68	64	69	71	82
30	61	62	63	66	72	82
40	62	63	64	67	75	89
50	-	-	-	-	-	-

Table 7.3: Elapse times for join method Index + Set Key=

# Columns Retrieved	% of Rows Retrieved					
	1%	5%	10%	20%	50%	100%
1	47	61	69	94	161	268
5	46	56	68	92	153	270
10	48	59	71	94	187	297
20	49	59	71	97	159	270
30	48	57	68	90	156	267
40	47	56	68	88	156	262
50	47	56	68	92	158	263

Table 7.4: Elapse times for join method Index + Sasfile + Set Key=

# Columns Retrieved	% of Rows Retrieved					
	1%	5%	10%	20%	50%	100%
1	49	53	53	58	72	93
5	50	52	55	59	71	96
10	55	58	60	66	77	99
20	61	63	67	72	82	105
30	63	66	68	73	87	110
40	68	71	72	78	94	118
50	-	-	-	-	-	-

The worst relative performance is achieved by sorting when few rows were needed, and by indexing when many rows are needed. This makes sense of course, and it is comforting that hard numbers confirm what one may intuitively deduce.

When we aggregate the best times from the tables above, we can see that each method has its place.

Table 7.5: Best elapse times for all join methods

# Columns Retrieved	% of Rows Retrieved						
	1%	5%	10%	20%	50%	100%	
1	47	53	53	58	65	73	Sort+merge
5	46	52	55	59	66	77	(sorted output)
10	48	58	60	66	69	80	Hash table
20	49	59	64	69	71	82	Index+set key=
30	48	57	63	66	72	82	Index+sasfile+key=
40	47	56	64	67	75	89	
50	47	56	68	92	105	110	

It is clear here that index lookups are the fastest when few rows are needed.

When fetching more rows, loading data in memory accelerates the random reads, with SASFILE having an edge for fewer columns, and a hash table being better for more columns.

For the last row of the test (50 columns retrieved), the only available methods are indexing and sorting since the lookup table cannot be loaded in memory.

In this case, sorting becomes better when more than 20% of the rows are fetched.

Now, if the tables are already sorted and/or indexed, the results are markedly different. When the data is prepared and stored in a ready-to-use and optimised manner, merging is always the fastest, unless one percent or less of the rows is retrieved. In the latter case, using the index is the fastest way to retrieve data.

Table 7.6: Elapse times (prepared data) for method Sort + Merge by

# Columns Retrieved	% of Rows Retrieved					
	1%	5%	10%	20%	50%	100%
1	32	32	33	33	32	32
5	33	33	32	32	32	32
10	34	34	35	36	34	35
20	36	36	36	36	35	35
30	37	38	38	38	37	37
40	38	38	38	39	39	39
50	40	41	41	41	41	41

Table 7.7: Elapse times (prepared data) for join method Hash table

# Columns Retrieved	% of Rows Retrieved					
	1%	5%	10%	20%	50%	100%
1	57	59	58	60	65	73
5	56	57	59	61	66	77
10	61	63	64	69	69	80
20	66	68	64	69	71	82
30	61	62	63	66	72	82
40	62	63	64	67	75	89
50	-	-	-	-	-	-

Table 7.8: Elapse times (prepared data) for join method Index + Set Key=

# Columns Retrieved	% of Rows Retrieved					
	1%	5%	10%	20%	50%	100%
1	33	42	54	78	145	254
5	32	41	52	77	139	255
10	33	44	56	78	171	281
20	33	43	56	81	145	255
30	33	42	53	75	142	252
40	32	42	53	74	142	248
50	32	41	53	77	142	248

Table 7.9: Elapse times (prepared data) for join method Index + Sasfile + Set Key=

# Columns Retrieved	% of Rows Retrieved					
	1%	5%	10%	20%	50%	100%
1	35	37	38	42	56	78
5	35	37	39	44	56	81
10	40	43	45	50	62	86
20	46	48	51	63	67	90
30	48	51	53	58	73	95
40	53	57	57	63	80	103
50	-	-	-	-	-	-

Table 7.10: Best elapse times (prepared data) for all join methods

# Columns Retrieved	% of Rows Retrieved						
	1%	5%	10%	20%	50%	100%	
1	32	32	33	33	32	32	Sort+merge
5	32	33	32	32	32	32	(sorted output)
10	33	34	35	36	34	35	Index+set key=
20	33	36	36	36	35	35	
30	33	38	38	38	37	37	
40	32	38	38	39	39	39	
50	32	41	41	41	41	41	

In case the run times of various methods are similar (or even if merging is somewhat slower), I would always favour the merging technique since it generates a sorted table, whereas using an index does not necessarily do so. So in practical terms, I would never use indexes for this latter test as I believe that a sorted table is much more useful than a few seconds saved.

If only SAS had an option to set the SORT VALIDATED flag when a merged table is created!

Note how merging is indifferent to the number of rows retrieved and only varies with the number of columns –since merging always retrieve all rows regardless of how many are kept-, while using the index is only influenced by the number of rows retrieved. That's because all the clock time is spent seeking the data, and once the data is found, reading one single observation's data takes a negligible amount of time.

The other two methods (hash and SASFILE), which carry the overhead of loading the data in memory before starting to use it, are inadequate in this example. This overhead is never offset by subsequent savings.

The second part of the benchmark, where the tables are already sorted and/or indexed, should convince you that storing the data sets in ready-to-use shape, by sorting and/or indexing them (and setting the SORT VALIDATED flag) - depending on the planned usage- pays off generous dividends.

Do not rely on SAS choosing when to use an index

SAS uses many parameters to decide on whether to use an index or not. This is true for joins, but can be demonstrated more simply via a where clause.

Let's create a 10-million row sample table and extract a portion of it using a where clause. We create an index on a numeric variable and one on a character variable, to see if they are used differently.

```
data TEST(index=(I C));
   do I=1 to 1e7; C=put(I,z10.); output; end;
run;
```

Now I extract a growing subset of the table while monitoring when SAS decides to stop using an index. Here are the transition values for that decision, for each of the numeric and the character index.

```
data _null_;set TEST;            * Fetch 5.6% of obs, Index is used
  where C > '0009440921';run;    real time= 0.25s ;

data _null_;set TEST;            * Fetch one more obs, Index not used
  where C > '0009440920';run;    real time= 0.98s;

data _null_;set TEST;            * Fetch 5.6% of obs, Index is used
  where I >  0009440775 ;run;    real time= 0.25s ;

data _null_;set TEST;            * Fetch one more obs, Index not used
  where I >  0009440774 ;run;    real time= 0.99s;
```

The data step stops using the index when around 5% of the table is extracted. Beyond this, a full-table scan is performed.

For our table, this cut-off point is too early, and we should be using the index for larger extracts. When the switchover occurs, the premature decision results in a quadrupling the run time.

The SAS optimiser chooses a slightly different cut-off point for numeric and character variables, but this makes no meaningful difference.

Interestingly, the logic used by SAS to derive the switchover point is completely different with PROC SQL.

PROC SQL uses the index until we try to extract around 40% of the table for the numeric variable, and 75% for the character variable. This is much too late, and as soon as we switchover by retrieving one fewer observation, the elapse time drop by 30% to 50%.

```
proc sql _method;create table T as select    * Index used, Fetch 40% of obs
count(*) from TEST where I > 0005942475;      real time= 1.8s ;

proc sql _method;create table T as select    * Index not used, Fetch one more obs
count(*) from TEST where I > 0005942474;      real time= 1.3s;

proc sql _method;create table T as select    * Index used, Fetch 75% of obs
```

166

`count(*) from TEST where C > '0002424226';`
 	
`proc sql` `_method;create table T as select`
`count(*) from TEST where C > '0002424225';`
	`real time= 3.4s ;`
	
	`* Index not used, Fetch one more obs`
	`real time= 1.8s;`

As you can see in the graph below, the optimal switchover point for this data is around 25% of record retrieved. Ignore the few peaks, the server was not quite idle when testing.

Figure 7.4: The switchover points set by SAS to decide when to use an index are not always optimal

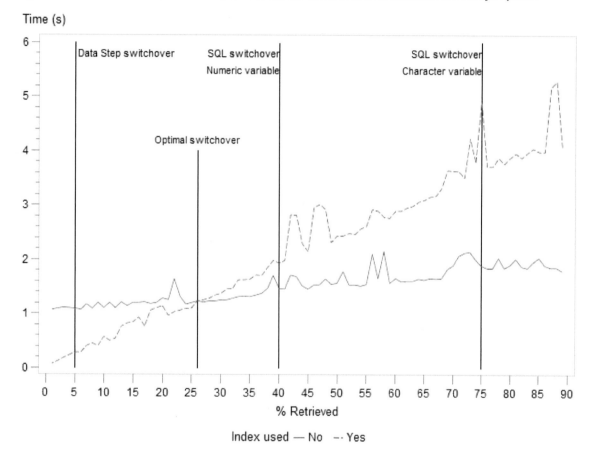

In conclusion, it is obvious that while SAS tries to find the best option, its guess is not always correct. Once the process you are putting in production is stabilised, you should decide whether an index should be used or not, and force SAS to uphold your decision. This is done by using the IDXWHERE= dataset option. This option can be used in the data step and with all procedures.

`create table T as select count(*) from`
`TEST(idxwhere=yes) where C > '0002424225';`
 	
`create table T as select count(*) from`
`TEST(idxwhere=no ) where C > '0002424226';`
	`* Force using the index`
	`real time= 3.3s;`
	
	`* Force not using the index`
	`real time= 1.7s;`

SQL "fuzzy" joins

One of SQL's strong points when it comes to joining tables is that SQL can perform fuzzy joins, i.e. it can join on more than just exact key values.

A data step can only do equijoins, where the keys are exactly equal. SQL can accept unequal keys and join on almost any criterion, including for example intervals or arithmetic difference or spelling distance or characters contained in strings. While this versatility allows for powerful algorithms, it can very quickly degrade performance as these fuzzy joins often generate a Cartesian product of the input tables.

There are ways to counter this however, and we can use equijoins to limit the scope of the potential matches and transform one single large Cartesian product into many much smaller Cartesian products.

Here are two examples demonstrating the performance gains obtained by using equijoins to restrict the scope of the fuzzy joins. One uses a join on strings while the other uses a join on numbers.

The first example mimics a classic task: we want to find keywords present in a list of phrases.

The test creates three tables: a list of (made-up, random) words. This table used to create the other two tables: a list of keywords, and a list of phrases that may or may or may not contain the keywords.

We then join the keyword table to the phrase table, looking for any phrase that contains any of the keywords.

The first test does this in a straightforward manner and simply uses the index function or the like operator to find matches.

The second test is more convoluted and requires a couple more steps but is overall much faster.

To accelerate the join, we extract each word from the phrase table to create an intermediate table with one observation per word. We can then use an equijoin to match each phrase word to a keyword, and then left join to retrieve the original phrase.

For this test, we try to find one thousand keywords in 1 million sentences.

Example 1: Finding one thousand keywords in 1 million sentences.

```
%* Create test data: List of words, and list of keywords to look for ;
data WORDS    (keep=WORD)
     KEYWORDS(keep=WORD rename=(WORD=KEYWORD));
  length WORD $8;
  do I=1 to 1e5;
    WORD=' ';
    do J= 1 to 8;
      WORD=catt(WORD,byte(ranuni(0)*90+32 ));
    end;
    output WORDS;
    if ranuni(0) > .99 then output KEYWORDS;
  end;
run;

%* Create test data: List of phrases ;
sasfile WORDS load;
data PHRASES (keep=PHRASE);
  length PHRASE $120;
  do I=1 to 1e6;
    PHRASE=' ';
    do J=1 to 15;
      KEY=ranuni(0)*1e5;
      set WORDS point=KEY;
      PHRASE=catx(' ',PHRASE,WORD);
    end;
    output PHRASES;
  end;
  stop;
run;
sasfile WORDS close;

%* Match method 1: brute force SQL, no equijoin, index function;
proc sql;
  create table MATCHES1 as
  select PHRASE, KEYWORD
  from PHRASES
      ,KEYWORDS
  where indexw(PHRASE,KEYWORD)
  order by PHRASE, KEYWORD;
quit;

%* Match method 1: brute force SQL, no equijoin, like operator;
proc sql;
  create table MATCHES1 as
  select PHRASE, KEYWORD
  from PHRASES
      ,KEYWORDS
  where PHRASE like '%'||trim(KEYWORD)||'%'
  order by PHRASE, KEYWORD;
quit;

/*
The index function and the like operator yield similar results.
NOTE: Table WORK.MATCHES1 created, with 19751 rows and 2 columns.
      real time          31.67 seconds
      user cpu time      31.43 seconds
*/
```

```
%*** Match method 2: equijoin;
%*   Step 1: create a list of phrase words, and create a foreign key for each phrase;
data PHRASES     (keep=OBSNO PHRASE )
     PHRASE_WORDS(keep=OBSNO WORD   );
  set PHRASES ;
  length WORD $10;
  OBSNO=_N_;
  do I= 1 to 15;
    WORD=scan(PHRASE,I,' ');
    output PHRASE_WORDS;
  end;
  output PHRASES;
run;
%*      real time            0.84 seconds;

%*   Step 2: Deduplicate in case a phrase contains the same word twice;
proc sort data=PHRASE_WORDS nodupkey;
  by WORD OBSNO;
run;
%*      real time            0.82 seconds;

%*   Step 3: Equi-join on keywords and retrieve matching phrase;
proc sql;
  create table MATCHES2 as
  select PHRASE, KEYWORD
  from PHRASE_WORDS
        inner join
       KEYWORDS
         on PHRASE_WORDS.WORD=KEYWORDS.KEYWORD
         left join
       PHRASES
         on PHRASE_WORDS.OBSNO=PHRASES.OBSNO
  order by PHRASE, KEYWORD;
quit;
/*
NOTE: Table WORK.MATCHES2 created, with 19751 rows and 2 columns.
      real time          0.51 seconds
      user cpu time      0.46 seconds
*/
```

By using an equijoin, the run time drops from 30 seconds to 2 seconds.

Transforming our code to only use equijoins made it very efficient.

Let's now look at another common example, this time with numerical data. This second test involves two tables with geographical coordinates (latitude and longitude); we want to find points from the two tables which are within 20 kilometres of each other.

Example 2: Finding points which are within 20 kilometres of each other.

The function GEODIST is very useful here and gives us the distance between the two coordinates, but matching all the points using just this function generates an expensive Cartesian product.

We can limit the size of the Cartesian product by using an intermediate table that contains a few acceptable rounded values for the difference in latitude, and perform equijoins on this table. This reduces the number of possible matches that the GEODIST function must evaluate.

```
data TAB1(keep  =POINT LAT1 LON1
          rename=(POINT=POINT1))
     TAB2(keep  =POINT LAT2 LON2
          rename=(POINT=POINT2));
  do POINT= 1 to 1e4;
   LAT1 = ranuni(0)*180-90;
   LON1 = ranuni(0)*360-180;
   LAT2 = ranuni(0)*180-90;
   LON2 = ranuni(0)*360-180;
   output ;
  end;
run;

%*1;proc sql _method stimer;
  create table MATCH1 as
  select *
 ,geodist(LAT1,LON1,LAT2,LON2) as DIST
  from TAB1, TAB2
  where calculated DIST < 20; quit;

%*2;proc sql _method stimer;
  create table MATCH2 as
  select *
 ,geodist(LAT1,LON1,LAT2,LON2) as DIST
  from TAB1, TAB2
  where abs(LAT1-LAT2)<.25
     and calculated DIST < 20; quit;

%*3;data LATDIFF ;
  DIFF=-0.25; output;
  DIFF= 0   ; output;
  DIFF= 0.25; output;
run;
proc sql _method stimer;
  create table MATCH3 as
  select *
 ,geodist(LAT1,LON1,LAT2,LON2) as DIST
  from TAB1, TAB2, LATDIFF
  where round(LAT1 ,0.25) = DIFF +
round(LAT2 ,0.25)
     and calculated DIST < 20; quit;
```

```
%* Create test data: 2 tables containing
coordinates;




%*** Match method 1: Brute force SQL, no
equijoin, geodist function only;

NOTE: Table WORK.MATCH1 created, with 722
rows and 7 columns.
       real time          1:13.15
       user cpu time      1:12.71

%*** Match method 2: Brute force SQL, no
equijoin, use the latitude difference
criterion without equijoin;

NOTE: Table WORK.MATCH2 created, with 722
rows and 7 columns.
       real time          1:20.51
       user cpu time      1:18.35

%*** Match method 3: Use the latitude
difference criterion in an equijoin;

NOTE: Table WORK.MATCH3 created, with 722
rows and 8 columns.
       real time          0.34 seconds
```

We can see here the extraordinary benefit of avoiding a full Cartesian product thanks to the use of an intermediate equijoin. The new join is so efficient that can have 100,000 points in both tables instead of 10,000, and still be faster than the brute-force join on the small table.

```
%* 1e5 points ;
NOTE: Table WORK.MATCH3 created, with 82210 rows and 8 columns.
      real time          37.45 seconds
```

Another note about equi-joins

Sometimes, one might assume that equi-joins are used when they are not. One such time is when using the OR operator. Consider the following example:

```
data TEST;
  do I=1 to 1e4;
    output;
  end;
run;

proc sql;
  create table T as
  select t1.I
  from TEST t1,TEST t2          real time            0.01 seconds
  where t1.I = t2.I ;           user cpu time        0.01 seconds
quit;

proc sql;
  create table T as             NOTE: The execution of this query involves
  select t1.I                   performing one or more Cartesian product
  from TEST t1,TEST t2          joins that can not be optimized.
  where t1.I = t2.I                 real time            3.45 seconds
    | t1.I = t2.I;                  user cpu time        3.43 seconds
quit;
```

Here, adding the OR operator transformed the equi-join into a Cartesian product. A note to that effect is visible in the LOG. Always scan the LOG for unexpected notes to avoid such catastrophic performance degradation.

A circumvention for the issue in this example is to remove the OR clause and to split the join into equi-joins. This restores performance.

```
proc sql;

  create table T as
  select t1.I
  from TEST t1,TEST t2
  where < condition 1 >

  union all

  select t1.I
  from TEST t1,TEST t2
  where < condition 2 >

quit;
```

Join methods used by PROC SQL, and relevant options

When joining tables, PROC SQL uses its own secret algorithm to decide when to sort tables, when to load them in a hash table or when use indexes if they exist. There are many factors used to make this decision, and the result is not always as expected. The main factors are:

- How much memory is left for PROC SQL to use when the query is run
- The value of the JOINTECH_PREF option
- The use of the IDXWHERE option
- The size of the columns in the tables that participate in the join
- Whether the tables are sorted on one or more of the join key columns
- Whether there are any indexes, on the join key columns
- The estimated cardinality of the predicates that are specified for the join

The choice made is sometimes puzzling and cannot be easily altered except by using the unreliable PROC SQL option MAGIC=. Look up this option to know more.

I recommend that you read technical paper TS-553 titled "SQL Joins – The Long and The Short of It" by Paul Kent (current URL *https://support.sas.com/techsup/technote/ts553.html*) to know more about PROC SQL's decision making. It is a bit dated (for example, PROC SQL option BUFFERSIZE is replaced by the confusingly-named option UBUFSIZE –nothing to do with its SAS general option namesake - in recent versions of SAS, and the buffer size is now dynamic), but most of its contents is still very relevant. The information surfaced by the option _METHOD is also explained in this paper.

PROC SQL's behaviour is still a bit of a mysterious black box, and trial and error seems to be the best way to peek under the hood. Here is an example of how the UBUFSIZE option influences performance. In this example, leaving the default UBUFSIZE setting increases run time by 50% while using more memory.

```
data TAB1 TAB2;                          %* Create test data;
  length A $80;
  do I=1 to 1e7;
    KEY=int(ranuni(0)*1e15);
    output;
  end;                                   %* Default setting, ubufsize unknown but around 50m.
run;                                          sqxsort method chosen
                                              real time          34.75
proc sql _method ;                            memory             1179375.95k
  create table TEST as
  select TAB1.*, TAB2.A as B
  from TAB1, TAB2
  where TAB1.KEY=TAB2.KEY;
quit;
                                         %* Set ubufsize to 50m.
proc sql _method buffersize=50m;              Same result as above;
  create table TEST as
  select TAB1.*, TAB2.A as B
  from TAB1, TAB2
  where TAB1.KEY=TAB2.KEY;
quit;
```

```
proc sql _method buffersize=80m;      %* Set ubufsize to 80m.
  create table TEST as                Memory usage *decreases* while performance improves.
  select TAB1.*, TAB2.A as B          proc SQL has now enough memory to use a hash table
  from TAB1, TAB2                     join.
  where TAB1.KEY=TAB2.KEY;               sqxjhsh method chosen
quit;                                    real time        22.78 seconds
                                         memory           1224563.62k;
```

The default is clearly not the best value here.

Just as for the for the index switchover threshold, it pays to force this option once your jobs are stable and ready for production.

Merging *and* appending.

Here is a situation I encountered a few times: There are monthly customer snapshot tables, and additional monthly tables containing further customer information. Now we need 10 years of history to build a model, and the information needed is in both in the main tables and in the additional ones. So there are 240 to tables to join, both horizontally (one row contains standard and additional information for one customer for one month) and vertically (120 months).

Here is a mock-up of this test, with just 100,000 records (i.e. 100,000 customers).

```
%let month_nb=120;

%macro sample_data;
  %local month_no;
  %do month_no=1%to &month_nb.;
    data DATA1_MTH&month_no. (keep=CUST_NO EVENT MTH_NO INFO1-INFO25)
         DATA2_MTH&month_no. (keep=CUST_NO       MTH_NO INFO26-INFO50) ;
      retain INFO1-INFO50 1 MTH_NO &month_no. ;
      do CUST_NO=1 to 1e5;
        EVENT=(ranuni(0)<.01);
        output;
      end;
    run;
  %end;
%mend;
%sample_data;


data JOIN1;                * Elapse time: 15 min;
  merge DATA1_MTH1-DATA1_MTH&month_nb.
        DATA2_MTH1-DATA2_MTH&month_nb.;
  by MTH_NO CUST_NO;
run;
```

In this data step, SAS opens all 240 tables and for each row scan each of them to see which ones contribute. There has to be a better way. To improve this join, we must tell SAS to read the table in a sensible manner.

One way to optimise the join is to have all the main customer tables appended together as one long vertical table, and all the additional customer tables appended together as well. This way we have a standard 2-table merge. Because the volume of the data makes this impractical and expensive, we create two views instead.

Creation of two vertical views:

```
%macro create_viewsV;
  data _VV1/view=_VV1;
    set DATA1_MTH1-DATA1_MTH&month_nb.;
  run;
  data _VV2/view=_VV2;
    set DATA2_MTH1-DATA2_MTH&month_nb.;
  run;
%mend;
%create_viewsV
```

Merging these two views yields a massive improvement, despite the overhead that views carry.

```
data JOIN2;            * Elapse time: 107s / CPU time: 43s;
  merge _VV1 _VV2;
  by MTH_NO CUST_NO;
run;
```

In this configuration SAS still has to open all the tables at once to perform this join. How about we allowed SAS to only have two active tables at any time? Let's create 120 horizontal joins (one per month) of only two tables. That's a bit more complex as we create 120 views, but only one view at a time is active, and only two tables are open at any time.

```
%macro create_viewsH;
  %local month_no;
  %do month_no=1 %to &month_nb.;
    data _VH&month_no./view=_VH&month_no.;
      merge DATA1_MTH&month_no. DATA2_MTH&month_no. ;
      by CUST_NO;
    run;
  %end;
%mend;
%create_viewsH
```

This configuration brings more even more structure to the join as SAS only deals with two tables at once.

```
data JOIN3;            * Elapse time: 47s / CPU time: 40s;
  set _VH1-_VH120;
run;
```

This example shows a further valuable improvement. It really does pay to organise joins.

The gains in this example are realised despite SAS views having a very expensive overhead. How high is this overhead?

Views have a costly overhead

We had a first look at views in Chapter 3. We can look again here.

How much performance is lost when using SAS views? Quite a bit, and views should only be used as a last resort. Let's quantify the cost of views by reading the customer data created above directly, and then through one of the view. For this comparison, we use the vertical view with 120 tables which is defined above, and compare with reading the tables directly.

```
data _null_;        * Elapse time: 18s / CPU time: 10s;
  set _VV1;
run;

data _null_;        * Elapse time: 9s / CPU time: 8s;
  set DATA1_MTH1 - DATA1_MTH&month_nb.;
run;
```

Here, using a view doubles the elapse time. The high cost of using SAS views makes them a poor option most times, but there are cases where they make a positive difference.

Joining a large number of data sets

One reason we could speed up the query above is that SAS becomes very inefficient when processing hundreds of tables concurrently with a BY statement, and the elapse (and CPU) time grows exponentially as more tables are added.

When possible, it is much faster to split the processing. This can be done as above by making smarter use of the data structure, or simply as below, by cutting the job into smaller pieces.

The SET statement is even more prone to "table overload" than the MERGE statement. Note how small the tables are here (2,000 observations only), and how quickly the elapse times soar.

```
%*********** C R E A T E   S A M P L E  ***********;
%let nbobs=2000;
%let nbtab=1000;

%* Create sample tables;
data     %macro loop; %local i; %do i=1 %to &nbtab.;
    HAVE&i.(rename=(J=J&i. K=K&i. L=L&i. M=M&i.) compress=no where=(I<3 or
I>&i.))
         %end; %mend; %loop;
  do I=1 to &nbobs.;
    J=I;K=I;L=I;M=I;
    output;
  end;
run;
```

```
%*********** M E R G E   B Y ************;
%* merge 100 tables ==> 0.7 seconds;
data WANT;  merge HAVE1-HAVE100;  by I;  run;

%* merge 200 tables ==> 2 seconds;
data WANT;  merge HAVE1-HAVE200;  by I;  run;

%* merge 500 tables ==> 15 seconds;
data WANT;  merge HAVE1-HAVE500;  by I;  run;

%* merge 1000 tables ==> 65 seconds;
data WANT;  merge HAVE1-HAVE1000; by I;  run;

%* Break merge in 200-table blocks ==> total time 10 seconds;
data T1; merge   HAVE1 - HAVE200;  by I; run;
data T2; merge HAVE201 - HAVE400;  by I; run;
data T3; merge HAVE401 - HAVE800;  by I; run;
data T4; merge HAVE601 - HAVE800;  by I; run;
data T5; merge HAVE801 -HAVE1000;  by I; run;
data T6; merge T1-T5;  by I; run;



%************* S E T   B Y *************;
%* set 50 tables ==> 4 seconds;
data WANT;  set HAVE1-HAVE50;  by I;  run;

%* set 100 tables ==> 26 seconds;
data WANT;  set HAVE1-HAVE100;  by I;  run;

%* set 200 tables ==> 180 seconds!;
data WANT;  set HAVE1-HAVE200;  by I;  run;

%* Break set in 40-table blocks ==> total time 9 seconds;
data T1; set   HAVE1 -  HAVE40; by I; run;
data T2; set  HAVE49 -  HAVE80; by I; run;
data T3; set  HAVE89 - HAVE120; by I; run;
data T4; set HAVE129 - HAVE160; by I; run;
data T5; set HAVE159 - HAVE200; by I; run;
data T6; set T1-T5;  by I; run;
```

I don't have an explanation to offer as to why performance drops so sharply when a large number of tables is used, and SAS could certainly optimize the way multiple opened tables are managed. In any case do keep this in mind.

Deleting records using a lookup table

It is often faster to recreate a data set rather than flagging some records as deleted.

On one hand, recreating the dataset has the advantage of recovering the space previously used by deleted observations.

On the other hand, recreating the dataset may not be desirable because it destroys the metadata or because it can prevent auditing. For large tables, deleting individual records may also be faster.

The example below compares recreating a table to deleting a single observation using the MODIFY statement or PROC SQL's delete statement. The least efficient methods are shown first.

```
/* create sample data                              */
data TEST(index=(J)); do I=1 to 1e7; J=I; output; end; run;


/* full scan, index not used - real time = 6.4  seconds*/
data TEST; modify TEST;      if J=9999997 then remove; run;

/* full scan, no index      - real time = 6.3  seconds*/
data TEST; modify TEST;      if I=9999996 then remove; run;

/* full scan, rewrite       - real time = 4.5  seconds*/
data TEST1; set TEST;        if I=9999995 then delete; run;

/* full scan+where, no index  - real time = 3.5  seconds*/
data TEST; modify TEST;      where I=9999993 ; remove; run;

/* full scan+where, no index  - real time = 3.4  seconds*/
proc sql; delete from TEST   where I=9999994 ; quit;

/* random access, index used - real time = 0.01 seconds*/
data TEST; modify TEST;      where J=9999992 ; remove; run;

/* random access, index used - real time = 0.01 seconds*/
proc sql; delete from TEST  where J=9999991; quit;
```

In this case, PROC SQL or MODIFY are the fastest when a WHERE clause is used together with an index. Next are the deletions using WHERE with no index, followed by a total overwrite, and last is a full table scan using an IF statement.

As usual, increasing the number of records to delete will make the index lose its lead, until a full table scan becomes the fastest option.

☞ Note that using a function (for example ROUND) rather than an equality prevents using the indexes.

If we delete more records by matching a lookup table, we can do a richer comparison.

Let us delete 0.1%, 1% and 10% of the rows in a 10 million-row table.

```
/* create sample data     1e5 and 1e7                      .9 .99 and .999  */
data MAIN UPD; do I=1 to 1e7; output MAIN; if ranuni(1)>.9 then output UPD; end; run;

/* 1. data step modify by            */
data MAIN; modify MAIN UPD; by I; if _IORC_=0 then remove; else output; run;

/* 2. sql delete exists()            */
proc sql; delete from MAIN where exists (select 1 from UPD where MAIN.I=UPD.I); quit;

/* 3. sql delete in()               */
proc sql; delete from MAIN where I in (select I from UPD); quit;

/* 4. data step modify with hash        */
data MAIN; modify MAIN;  if _n_=1 then do;
  dcl hash h1(dataset:'UPD'); h1.defineKey('I'); h1.defineDone(); end;
  if h1.check()=0 then remove; run;

/* 5. datastep rewrite table hash       */
data MAIN; set MAIN; if _n_=1 then do;
  dcl hash h1(dataset:'UPD'); h1.defineKey('I'); h1.defineDone(); end;
  if h1.check()=0 then delete; run;

/* 6. data step modify with key= (requires an index on table MAIN) */
data MAIN; set UPD; modify MAIN key=I;
   if _IORC_= %sysrc(_sok) then remove; else _ERROR_=0; run;

/* 7. sql rewrite table             */
proc sql; create table MAIN1 as select MAIN.*
  from MAIN left join UPD on MAIN.I=UPD.I where UPD.I is null order by I; quit;

/* 8. data step update by           */
data MAIN; update MAIN UPD(in=UPD); by I; if UPD then delete; run;

/* 9. Data step rewrite table merge by */
data MAIN; merge MAIN UPD(in=UPD); by I; if UPD then delete; run;
```

Table 7.11: Elapse times when deleting records using a lookup table

Lookup method	100k obs. Delete 10%	10m obs. Delete 10%	10m obs. Delete 1%	10m obs. Delete 0.1%
data step modify by	140	-	-	-
sql delete exists()	24	-	-	-
sql delete in()	0	16.0	11.17	9.2
data step modify + hash	0	13.0	9.3	8.7
data step set + hash	0	6.0	3.5	2.8
data step modify key=	0	5.0	1.3	0.2
sql rewrite	0	3.4	3.1	2.9
data step update by	0	1.9	1.9	1.8
data step merge by	0	1.9	1.8	1.6

The first two methods were only tested on a small table because they are so slow. We can see again how inefficient the data step's MODIFY BY statement is. Likewise, SQL's `exists` operator is best avoided as it can trigger one subquery for every row of the main table.

When performing a full-table rewrite, PROC SQL is slower than either data step methods.

When few records are updated, MODIFY + KEY= is the fastest by far.

PROC SQL's merge speed (test #7) for the rewrite test can be improved (this is not shown here) by sorting the input tables (i.e. by setting the SORT VALIDATED flag), but never matches the speed of a data step.

Remember that using an index becomes more and more preferable as the proportion of observations targeted decreases, and as the length of the observation increases.

Updating records from a lookup table

A similar test can be conducted to update (rather than delete) records in a table, and yields similar results.

```
/* create sample data    1e5 and 1e7                          .9 .99 and .999  */
data MAIN UPD; do I=1 to 1e7; J=I; output MAIN; J+1; if ranuni(1)>.9 then output UPD; end;
run;

/* 1. data step modify by */
data MAIN; modify MAIN UPD; by I; if _IORC_=0 then replace; else output;run;

/* 2. sql update          */
proc sql; update MAIN set J=(select J from UPD where MAIN.I=UPD.I) where I in (select I
from UPD); quit;

/* 3. sql rewrite         */
proc sql; create table MAIN1 as select MAIN.I, coalesce(UPD.J, MAIN.J) as J from MAIN left
join UPD on MAIN.I=UPD.I order by 1; quit;

/* 4. data step modify with index */
data MAIN; set UPD(rename=(J=J1)); modify MAIN key=I;
   if _IORC_= %sysrc(_sok) then do; J=J1; replace; end; else _ERROR_=0; run;

/* 5. data step update    */
data MAIN; update MAIN UPD; by I; run;

/* 6. data step rewrite   */
data MAIN1; merge MAIN UPD; by I; run;
```

Table 7.12: Elapse times when updating records using a lookup table

Lookup method	100k obs. Update 10%	10m obs. Update 10%	10m obs. Update 1%	10m obs. Update 0.1%
data step modify by	178	-	-	-
sql update in()	8	-	-	-
sql rewrite	0	7.0	6.8	6.2
data step modify key=	0	7.3	1.4	0.4
data step update by	0	5.9	5.8	5.4
data step merge by	0	5.8	5.5	5.2

Once more, MODIFY BY statement shines by its inefficiency. I reckon that something is not quite right in its implementation.

PROC SQL's update ... from ... select ... statement needs a convoluted syntax in SAS, and pays the price through poor performance.

The other results are similar to the deletion benchmark.

Don't forget that results will vary depending on your data. The wider the table, the costlier rewriting the table (MERGE BY) will be compared to just scanning it (UPDATE BY) and even more compared to using an index (MODIFY KEY=).

Below is a comparison of the last (best) four methods as the observation length of the MAIN table increased. The table above has a length of 16 bytes (two 8-bytes variables). If we conduct the same test with 200-byte and 2000-byte observation lengths, we can confirm the importance of picking the best method depending on table width. For small updates (in terms of percentage of observations), sorting only beats using an index if the observations are short and the size of the update is large (third panel below).

Also note that PROC SQL performs very poorly because the table does not include any metadata about the sort order, so PROC SQL sorts the table before merging. If the sort order is confirmed, times are similar to a data steps, though not quite as good.

Figure 7.5: Table update times as observation length increases

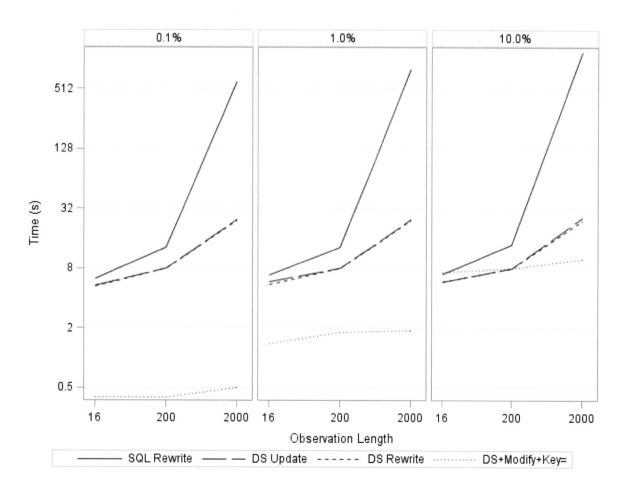

181

Flagging existing records from a lookup table using the EXISTS operator

The methods above used to delete or update records can also be used to flag records that exist in a lookup table.

There is no point repeating the tests above for that new purpose, but we'll focus on SQL's EXISTS operator, which is often used for this task, maybe due to its obvious name (let's use the EXISTS operator to check if something exists!).

Despite the enticing name, the results are similar as what we've seen before, and the EXISTS operator should generally be avoided for the purpose of looking up large tables.

``/* create sample data */
data MAIN LOOKUP;
  do I=1 to 1e5;
    output MAIN;
    if ranuni(0)>.9 then output LOOKUP;
  end;
run;

proc sql;
  create table MAIN as
  select MAIN.I,
exists(select 1 from LOOKUP where MAIN.I=LOOKUP.I) as FLG
  from MAIN;
quit;

proc sql;
  create table t4 as
  select MAIN.I, (LOOKUP.I is not null) as FLG
  from MAIN left join LOOKUP
  on MAIN.I=LOOKUP.I;
quit;``` | NOTE: PROCEDURE SQL used (Total process time):
    real time
24.45 seconds
    user cpu time
21.50 seconds
    system cpu time   2.71 seconds

NOTE: PROCEDURE SQL used (Total process time):
    real time   0.21 seconds
    user cpu time   0.06 seconds
    system cpu time   0.01 seconds |

A table join is much faster than using the EXIST operator. This operator should be used very sparingly.

Keeping only the records matching a lookup table using a nested SELECT statement

This next test is similar to the previous tests and the various methods yield comparable results.

I only added this section to focus on SQL's IN() operator.

Just as the EXISTS operator is often favoured to test for the existence of a value, the IN() operator with a nested SELECT is often used to subset a table.

This operator is slow however, and it is often better to use a join. The best usage for a nested a SELECT statement is when a very small number of values are sought.

If the source data is sorted, a data set MERGE shines by its speed once again. And it produces a sorted output, which is a useful bonus.

```
data MAIN LOOKUP;
  do ID=1 to 1e7;
  output MAIN;
  if ranuni(0)>.99 then output LOOKUP;
  end;
run;

proc sql;                    * in (select …) real time   4.79 seconds;
  create table WANT as
  select ID
  from MAIN
  where ID in (select ID from LOOKUP);
quit;

proc sql;                    * left join    real time   2.29 seconds;
  create table WANT as
  select main.*
  from MAIN
  left join LOOKUP
  on main.ID =lookup.ID
  where lookup.ID is not missing;
quit;

data WANT;                   * merge by     real time   1.32 seconds;
  merge MAIN LOOKUP(in=LOOKUP);
  by ID;
  if LOOKUP;
run;
```

Fastest lookup techniques depending on the percentage of rows retrieved

We have seen in the previous examples that two of the most efficient techniques to retrieve lookup data are a data step with MERGE + BY or UPDATE + BY for large lookups, and a data step with MODIFY + KEY for smaller ones. We saw that for our data, using an index is slower if more than around 10% of the rows are retrieved.

We can make drill-down a bit more. Here is the overall comparison of the main methods depending on the size ratio between the main table and the lookup table.

Figure 7.6: Break-even point depending on the percentage of rows retrieved in the lookup table

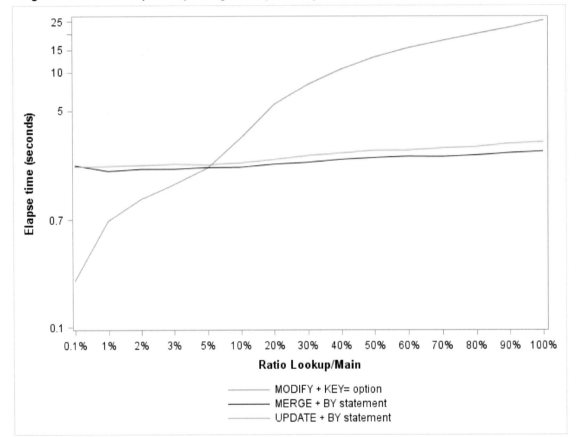

Note how the UPDATE method is always slightly faster than the MERGE method for our data.

The break-even point will of course move depending on the data and the hardware.

Here is the code used, in case you want to run this test on your machine:

```
%let lib=WORK;

options fullstimer msglevel=i compress=no nomprint nomlogic;

%macro loop;
         %*  1      2      3      4      5      6      7      8      9      10  ;
%let values=0.001  0.01   0.02   0.03   0.05   0.10   0.20   0.30   0.40   0.50
            0.60   0.70   0.80   0.90   1.00   ;

%do i=1 %to 15;
  %let j=%scan(&values,&i,%str( ));
data &lib..MASTER2
     &lib..MASTER3
     &lib..MASTER4
     &lib..TRANS ;
  do ID = 1 to 1e7 ;
    J=ID;
    output &lib..MASTER2
           &lib..MASTER3
           &lib..MASTER4;
    J+1;
    if ranuni(0) < &j. then output &lib..TRANS;
  end;
run;

%put ==> &=j;

proc sql;                              %* Building the index is a one-off cost.;
  create index ID on  &lib..MASTER2;   %* The index is retained.;
quit;
%put MODIFY + KEY= option;
data  &lib..MASTER2;
  set  &lib..TRANS(keep=ID);           %* Load key to modify;
  modify &lib..MASTER2 key=ID;         %* Load to record to modify;
  set  &lib..TRANS(drop=ID);           %* Load new data for key ;
  select(_IORC_);
    when(%sysrc(_sok)) replace;        %* Record found: Update in place;
    when(%sysrc(_dsenom)) output;      %* Record not found: Insert;
    otherwise ;
  end;
  _ERROR_=0;
run;

%put MERGE + BY statement;
data  &lib..MASTER3;                   %* Sorting cost if any is a one-off cost the 1st
time.;
  merge  &lib..MASTER3 &lib..TRANS;    %* The sorted order is then retained in the output
table.;
  by ID;
run;

%put UPDATE + BY statement;
data  &lib..MASTER4;                   %* The sorting cost if any is a one-off cost.;
  update &lib..MASTER4 &lib..TRANS;    %* The sorted order is retained.;
  by ID;
run;

%end;
%mend;
%loop;
```

Where is the data located?

This chapter would not be complete without a word about remote data, i.e. data not located on the SAS server doing the processing. What happens if you want to merge local data to remote data? At worst, a huge table will be transferred to the server doing the processing when only a small subset is needed.

Always be aware of the location of the data, and try to process it where is it. You can transfer only what you need, after that data has been subset or summarized or merged to other remote tables.

For example, if you query a RDBMS like Teradata or DB2 via SAS code (the SAS code does not have to use SQL), do not use SAS-specific functions like PUTN or INTNX to perform joins or to subset a table. Since these functions do not exist in DB2 (for example), they are not translated to DB2 functions and all the data must be transferred back to SAS where the function is then applied. Some functions such as SUBSTR are translated by SAS, but it is up to you to check this and to ensure that only the necessary data is moving across the network.

Some options available when writing SAS code, such as this syntax where a numeric field is used as a Boolean value: `where FLAG;` can yield surprises as SAS does not always translate properly to take into account both null and nil values.

If you need to aggregate a table, make sure this happens on the remote host, and only bring back the smaller summarised table. If you need to join remote tables, do it on the remote host as well.

You may have to use *Explicit pass-through* rather than *Implicit pass-through* to achieve the remote processing. Read about the difference between *Explicit pass-through* and *Implicit pass-through*, there are many good resources on the web. Learning database-specific language will help you.

To watch where the processing takes place, you can use the SASTRACE option. This option allows monitoring many things, including watching the exact queries sent to the database.

The same concerns apply if you use SAS's Remote Library Services. RLS allows you to see the data on a remote SAS session as if it was local. That's very handy for browsing it, but as soon as you must process it, you should remote-submit the code rather than submitting it locally and pointing to the local RLS library. If you run the code locally, all the tables used in the program are transferred to be processed, which will be inefficient in most cases. If you use SAS/CONNECT and RLS, familiarise yourself with these concepts.

Extract a subset of data hosted on a remote database

As an example of the challenges posed by accessing data on remote hosts, I picked another common task: extracting remote data based on a list of values stored on the local computer. Several methods are available to do this:

- If you are allowed to upload data and create remote tables, then it's easy: just upload the list as a table and perform a join on the remote server, before downloading only the data you need.

- If you cannot do this, the usual solution is to store the filter values inside one or several macro variables, and to run the extraction code on the server. The extraction code incorporates the filter as a list of hard-coded values in one or several IN() conditions(s), and only the data you need is brought back.
  A variant of this solution is the LIBNAME option `multi_datasrc_opt=in_clause` . This option manages the creation on the IN() list for you. Make sure to read about its limitations before using it though.

- A last solution for extracting a subset of a remote database table, provided the remote table is indexed on that value, is to use the DBKEY= option.

Here are the different methods put into use. In this example, we extract 2000 rows from a remote Teradata database.

First, we subset in SAS. This can be unfeasible if the remote table is large. This is the worst solution obviously.

Next, we use the DBKEY= option.

Then we upload the filter values in a macro variable.

Lastly, we use the MULTI_DATASRC_OPT=IN_CLAUSE option.

```
%* Create sample look-up values;
data LOOKUP; do I=1 to 2e3;
  ACCOUNT_ID=put(I,z10.); output; end;
run;

%* 1 - Match in SAS: Full download;
proc sql;
  create table T1 as select b.ACCOUNT_ID
  from LOOKUP a, DBLIB.ACCOUNTS b
  where a.ACCOUNT_ID = b.ACCOUNT_ID;

%* 2 - DBKEY= option;
proc sql;
  create table T4 as select b.ACCOUNT_ID
  from LOOKUP, DBLIB.ACCOUNTS(dbkey=ACCOUNT_ID) b
  where lookup.ACCOUNT_ID = b.ACCOUNT_ID;

%* 3 - In() list: Macro variable ;
proc sql noprint;
  select unique quote(trim(ACCOUNT_ID)) into
:values separated by ',' from LOOKUP;
  create table T2 as
  select ACCOUNT_ID
  from DBLIB.ACCOUNTS  b
  where ACCOUNT_ID in(&values.);

%* 4 - In() list: MULTI_DATASRC_OPT= option;
proc sql;
  create view _V as
  select b.ACCOUNT_ID
  from LOOKUP a, DBLIB.ACCOUNTS  b
  where a.ACCOUNT_ID = b.ACCOUNT_ID
  using libname DBLIB teradata user=xx ...
            multi_datasrc_opt=in_clause;
  create table T3 as select * from _V;
```

```
1 - Query sent to the database:
 SELECT "ACCOUNT_ID","MONTH_KEY"
FROM ACCOUNTS

NOTE: PROCEDURE SQL used (Total
process time):        real time
2:57.98

2 - 2000 queries sent to the
database:
  USING ("ACCOUNT_ID" VARCHAR
(22)) SELECT "ACCOUNT_ID" FROM
ACCOUNTS WHERE
"ACCOUNT_ID"=:"ACCOUNT_ID"

  NOTE: PROCEDURE SQL used (Total
process time):        real time
02:03:47.07

3 - Query sent to the database:
 SELECT "ACCOUNT_ID","MONTH_KEY"
FROM ACCOUNTS WHERE
("ACCOUNT_ID" IN ( '0000000001',
... 2000 values .. '0000002000'
))

  NOTE: PROCEDURE SQL used (Total
process time):        real time
23.00 seconds

4 - Query not visible in the log.

  NOTE: PROCEDURE SQL used (Total
process time):        real time
19.67 seconds
```

A full download is the least efficient, unsurprisingly.

The second slowest is using DBKEY=, but it's the easiest to code, and would be quite fast for just a few filter values.

Using macro variables is much faster, but not the fastest.

And the fastest is the option MULTI_DATASRC_OPT=IN_CLAUSE. It has limitations though, such its dependency on other options or a limit on the number of values that can be used, so familiarise yourself with it. This method does not display the remote query in the log window.

Accelerate the transfer between a remote database and SAS

When accessing a large volume of data on RDBMS, there are a few options to be aware of. These options are generally either LIBNAME options or data sets options. I could have added this section in the *Options* chapter, but I reckon they are more at home here.

This list is not meant to be exhaustive by any means. It is only here to give a glimpse of the rich set of configuration options that come with each SAS engine for a given database. Do read the documentation about the engines to the databases you are using.

READBUFF
Specifies the number of rows of DBMS data to read into memory
For reading remote data from Aster nCluster, DB2 under UNIX and PC Hosts, DB2 under z/OS, Greenplum, HP Neoview, Microsoft SQL Server, Netezza, ODBC, OLE DB, Oracle, Sybase, Sybase IQ

INSERTBUFF
Specifies the number of rows to insert in a DBMS in a single operation
For writing data into Aster nCluster, DB2 under UNIX and PC Hosts, Greenplum, HP Neoview, Microsoft SQL Server, MySQL, Netezza, ODBC, OLE DB, Oracle, Sybase IQ

BULKLOAD
Specifies whether SAS uses a DBMS facility to insert data into a DBMS table
For writing data into ODBC, OLE DB, Teradata

BULKUNLOAD
Specifies whether to use Netezza Remote External Table interface to read data

MULTILOAD, MULTI-STATEMENT, FASTLOAD, FBUFSIZE
Specifies whether to use the named Teradata utility to insert or append data

FASTEXPORT
Specifies whether to use the TPT API to read data from Teradata

BULKEXTRACT
Specifies whether to use HP Neoview Transporter when retrieving data

ENABLE_BULK
Specifies whether SAS performs a bulk copy into Sybase

So many options to discover. If performance is an issue when interfacing with your DBMS, dive into the documentation and head to the SAS communities web site. Get to know your software!

Conclusion

I hope that these few anecdotic examples will have presented some useful tips.

More importantly, I hope that exploring them will have given you a taste for stepping back and considering the numerous options and their consequences when joining tables.

Chapter 8

Regular Expressions

Introduction

Regular expressions are not intended to speed up SAS code. Rather they allow for compact code and complex text parsing.

The power of regular expressions makes comparing their execution speed with that of code using string functions both unfair and unfeasible. For simple string matching on short strings, regular expressions are typically slower than a few IF tests and common string function calls such as SUBSTR(), FIND(), LENGTH(). On longer strings the speed will match or exceed such IF test series. For more complex parsing, comparison becomes impossible as regular expressions can do so much more than text functions.

This power is the reason I decided to add this chapter. There is simply no replacement for the might of regular expressions, and if you manipulate strings, you must know the RegEx features that the SAS language supports.

I will not attempt to explain what each regular expression does, or what the SAS RegEx functions do, or give lengthy explanations about the syntax. Much excellent documentation exists that delves into these details, and there is not enough room in this book. Rather my goal here is to give a summary –or to provide a reminder– of most constructs, and to show the syntax available in SAS 9.4 to write and use a regular expression. Other regular expression constructs exist in various software packages that are not supported by SAS yet.

Documentation about the full features of regular expressions in SAS is scattered and sometimes incomplete or even inaccurate. I hope this summary and few examples can help the reader unleash their power.

Regular Expressions supported in SAS

Here is a list of the expressions that SAS supports, and some examples of their use as an aide-mémoire.

Expression	Description
Global structure	
/	Delimits the RegEx
m or s prefix	Specifies if the RegEx is for matching or substituting. m is implicit.
i suffix	Specifies that the RegEx is case insensitive.
x suffix	Specifies that the RegEx contains extended whitespace comments
s or m suffix	Specifies that the RegEx must use single- or multi- line treatment
	Multiline mode makes ^ and $ match the beginning and end of any line in the string, and not just the beginning and end of the string itself.
	Multiline is useful when passing multiple lines in a string while wanting to treat them as multiple lines (i.e. each starts with ^ and ends with $).
	Single-line is useful when passing multiple lines in a string while wanting to treat them as though they were a single line. See \z examples.
	In single-line mode, the dot matches everything including the line break.

	`POS=prxmatch('m/cats./ ' , 'cats'||'0a'x ); POS=0`
	`POS=prxmatch('m/cats./s' , 'cats'||'0a'x ); POS=1`
	`POS=prxmatch('m/cats./m' , 'cats'||'0a'x ); POS=0`

o suffix	Specifies to compile the RegEx once. This is the default in a DATA step, in a WHERE clause, or in PROC SQL, when a constant expression is used.
Matching	
Literal character	Any character except [\ ^ $. | ? * + ( ) matches an instance of itself
\	Escape character used to match special characters [\ ^ $. | ? * + ( ) as themselves. Other characters such as] { or # may also need to be escaped in some cases.
\d \D	Matches any (decimal: 0 to 9) digit. Matches anything but a decimal digit.
\w	Matches any word character (Latin letters including accented letters*, digits 0 to 9, underscore)
\W	Matches anything but a word character
\s \S	Matches a white space: HT (x09), LF (x0A), FF (x0C), CR (x0D), space (x20) Matches anything but a white space, including VT (x0B)
\0 \ddd	Matches an octal number ddd (3 digits max: 000 to 377)
\xdd \x{dd}	Matches a hexadecimal number dd (2 digits max: 00 to FF) Only the last 2 digits are taken into account if more than 2 digits.
\t	Matches a horizontal tab character. Same as \x09
\n	Matches a new line character. Same as \x0A
\r	Matches a carriage return character. Same as \x0D
\f	Matches a form feed character. Same as \x0C
\a	Matches a bell character. Same as \x07
\e	Matches an escape character. Same as \x1B

\cx	Matches Control+x where x is any letter A to Z or a to z.
	`* Match a Windows CRLF line break;`
	`POS=prxmatch('/\cM\cJ/', '0D0A'x); POS=1`

|	Pipe alternation metacharacter: allows several matching options `POS=prxmatch('/a|b/', 'cats'); POS=2 * Matches a;`
. (dot)	Matches any character at all except End-Of-Line x0A. If single-line mode is used, the dot matches x0A as well.

[]	Character set or character class: match any value in the list
	- Escaped matching characters like \d can be used and keep their meaning
	- Non-escaped characters like . or ? are simply treated as characters
	- The caret ^ in first position inverses the list.
	
	`* Find: not a digit, a ], a pipe, a lowercase letter;`
	`POS=prxmatch('/[^\d\]|a-z]/', '0]0A09');   POS=4`

Posix character classes	These are used as list items in character sets

Class	Description
[:alnum:]	letters and digits, identical to: a-zA-Z0-9 plus accented Latin letters*
[:alpha:]	letters, identical to: a-zA-Z plus accented Latin letters*
[:ascii:]	character codes 0 to 127, identical to: \x00-\x7F
[:blank:]	tab or space only, identical to: \x09\x20
[:cntrl:]	control characters, identical to: \x00-\x19
[:digit:]	decimal digits, identical to: \d
[:graph:]	printing characters, anything at all that uses ink
[:lower:]	lowercase letters, identical to: a-z plus accented Latin letters*
[:print:]	printing characters plus space
[:punct:]	printing characters excluding Latin letters and digits
[:space:]	white space (9=HT, 10= LF, 11=VT, 12=FF, 13=CR, 20=space), identical to \s plus VT
[:upper:]	uppercase letters, identical to: A-Z plus accented Latin letters*
[:word:]	word characters, identical to: \w
[:xdigit:]	hexadecimal digits, identical to 0-9a-fA-F

* The letters matched depend on the encoding. For example wlatin1 matches most Western Europe accents like ñ (Spanish) or ø (Swedish).

```
* Match 1 or 2 or any non-hexadecimal ;
PRX = prxparse("/[12[:^xdigit:]]/");
```

Iterator (or quantifier) metacharacters, laziness and greediness

?	? allows to match 0 or 1 occurrences of the preceding pattern.
+	+ allows to match 1 or more occurrences of the preceding pattern.
*	* allows to match 0 or more occurrences of the preceding pattern.

{}	The { } brackets allow to define exactly how many times the preceding pattern should be repeated.
	
	`PRX='\[a-zA-Z]{3}\ ';  * Match exactly 3 letters;`
	`PRX='\[a-zA-Z]{3,5}\';  * Match 3 to 5 letters;`
	`PRX='\[a-zA-Z]{3,}\ ';  * Match 3 or more letters;`

? for lazyness	By default, The * + ? { } metacharacters will select as many characters as possible to achieve a match.
	Adding ? behind the quantifier will make the match lazy instead of greedy.
	
	`STR='queue';`
	`PRX1=prxparse('/[aeiou]+/'     ); link match;  * LEN=4`
	`PRX1=prxparse('/[aeiou]{1,4}/' ); link match;  * LEN=4`
	`PRX1=prxparse('/[aeiou]+?/'    ); link match;  * LEN=1`
	`PRX1=prxparse('/[aeiou]{1,4}?/'); link match;  * LEN=4`
	`STR='A rooster, a cat, a dog, and a donkey.';`
	`PRX1=prxparse('/,.*,/' ); link match;       * LEN=15`
	`PRX1=prxparse('/,.*?,/'); link match;       * LEN=8`
	`match:`
	`call prxsubstr(PRX1, STR, POS, LEN);`

Capture groups	
( )	Capture group
(?:)	Non-capture group
\d \dd	Matches capture buffer *d* or *dd* in a search string (2 digits max: 1 to 99). Matches octal value if 2 digits and the backreference does not exist.

	`* First capture group is a, match is ada;`
	`POS=prxmatch(  '/(a|b)(c|d)\1/', 'adadd');   * POS=1`
	`* First capture group is d, match is add;`
	`POS=prxmatch('/(?:a|b)(c|d)\1/', 'adadd');   * POS=3`

$n $nn	Recall a capture group in a substitution
	`* Replace a or b with d plus match;` `STR=prxchange('s/(a|b)/d$1/', -1,'cats'); * STR=cdats`

Looking where we are in the string	
^	Zero-width assertion matching the beginning of a string or line
\A	Zero-width assertion matching the beginning of a string
$ \Z	Zero-width assertion matching the end of a string or new line (x0A)
\z	Zero-width assertion matching the end of a string only

	`STR='0a'x||'X'||'0a'x||'X'||'0a'x;`
	`POS=prxmatch('/ ^   X    /xm' , STR); * POS=2`
	`POS=prxmatch('/ ^   X    /x ' , STR); * POS=0`
	`POS=prxmatch('/ \A X    /xm' , STR); * POS=0`
	`POS=prxmatch('/ \A X    /x ' , STR); * POS=0`
	`POS=prxmatch('/    X  $ /xm' , STR); * POS=2`
	`POS=prxmatch('/    X  $ /x ' , STR); * POS=4`
	`POS=prxmatch('/    X \Z /xm' , STR); * POS=2`
	`POS=prxmatch('/    X \Z /x ' , STR); * POS=4`
	`POS=prxmatch('/    X \z /xm' , STR); * POS=0`
	`POS=prxmatch('/    X \z /x ' , STR); * POS=0`

\b	Zero-width assertion matching a word boundary (between \w and \W)
\B	Zero-width assertion matching anything but a word boundary
	`POS=prxmatch('/\ba/' , 'a cat'); * POS=1` `POS=prxmatch('/\Ba/' , 'a cat'); * POS=4`

\G	Zero-width assertion matching the previous match.
	The 9.4 documentation wrongly states that this is not supported.
	`STR = 'LIST1 A B C LIST2 C D E';`
	`PRX = prxparse("s/.*(LIST2|\G) (\w)+/$2|/");`
	`STR2= prxchange(PRX, -1, STR);`
	`STR2=C|D|E|`

(?=)	Zero-width positive look-ahead (look right) assertion.
(?!)	Zero-width negative look-ahead assertion.
(?<=)	Zero-width positive look-behind assertion (with fixed-width match string)

(?<!)	Zero-width negative look-behind assertion (with fixed-width match string)
	`data _null_;`
	`* Positive lookahead: Words followed by a S;`
	`REGEX= "/\b\w+ (?=S)/"; STR='Plug Slug'; link parse;`
	`* Negative lookahead: Words not followed by a S;`
	`REGEX= "/\b\w+ (?!S)/"; STR='Slug Plug'; link parse;`
	`* Positive lookbehind: Words ending with s;`
	`REGEX= "/\w+(?<=s)\b/"; STR='Plug Plus'; link parse;`
	`* Negative lookbehind: Words not ending with s;`
	`REGEX= "/\w+(?<!s)\b/"; STR='Plus Plug'; link parse;`
	`stop;`

```
parse:
PRX = prxparse(REGEX);
call prxsubstr(PRX, STR, POS, LEN);
putlog POS= LEN=;
run;
```

Test construct	

| (?(if)then\|else) | The match depends on a condition. |

The first test uses a look-around and toggles currency "informat."

The second test tries to match a then b. If a was found, it then tries to find a c otherwise a d.

(1) means that the capturing group number 1 matched.

```
data _null_;
* If currency=Yen, do not expect decimals;
PRX = prxparse("/(\$|¥)(?(?<=¥)\d+|\d+\.\d\d)/");
STR = '$53.36'; link parse; * read 2 decimals;
STR = '¥1345 '; link parse; * read integer;
* If group 1 'a' is matched, look for 'c';
PRX = prxparse("/(a)?b(?(1)c|d)/");
STR = 'abc   '; link parse; * match abc;
STR = 'abd   '; link parse; * match bd;
STR = 'bc    '; link parse; * no match;
STR = 'bd    '; link parse; * match bd;
* Optional balanced opening and closing parentheses;
PRX = prxparse("/ (\()? [^()]+ (?(1) \) ) /x");
STR = '(aa)  '; link parse; * match (aa);
stop;
parse:
call prxsubstr(PRX, STR, POS, LEN);
putlog POS= LEN=;
run;
```

Comments and inline modifiers	
(?#)	Comment: Anything in these brackets is ignored. `POS=prxmatch('/\d(?# digit)/', '1'); * POS=1`
\l	Lowercase the next character
\u	Uppercase the next character `POS=prxmatch('/(\ut)/','T');    * POS=1`
\L	Lowercase till \E
\U	Uppercase till \E
\Q	Quote regular expression metacharacters till \E `POS=prxmatch('/\Q\d\E/','\d'); * POS=1`

\E	End of case modification or quoting
	The inline modifiers can be used in character sets and in substitutions:
	`* Match any case c or d and uppercase it;`
	`STR = prxchange('s/([\LCD\E])/\U$1\E/',1,'bc'); STR=bC`

(?ixsm)
(?-i-x-s-m)
	Embedded pattern-matching modifiers to toggle case sensitivity, extended whitespace comments, single-line treatment, multiline treatment
	`POS=prxmatch('/(?i)Tt(?-i)/','TT');`
	`POS=prxmatch('/(?x) \ #space \w #word/', '1 C'); POS=2`

Regular Expressions in informats

Regular expressions can be used to define informats in order to read strings or even to transform them on the fly as they are read.

For example we can directly read the decimal numbers (we'll round them on the fly), integers, times, and dates from this text:

```
01jun12
3.
-4.9
text
113:34:33.22
9:3:3.8
03noviembre2012
Meeting at 14:30 sharp
```

And get the output:

```
Date 01JUN2012
Num      3.0000
Num     -5.0000
Num         .
Time 113:34:33.22
Time   9:03:03.80
Date 03NOV2012
Time   14:30:00.00
```

```
proc format;

  invalue anynum (default=24)
  's/.*?                 (?# lazy match of any character     )
    (                    (?# capture group                   )
      (\d+:)?            (?# [optional hours]                )
      \d{1,2}:           (?# [minutes]                       )
      \d{1,2}            (?# [seconds]                       )
      (\.\d+)?           (?# then optionally a dot and digits )
    )                    (?# end of capture group            )
    \D*                  (?# then optionally other characters )
  /\1/x'                 %*   only keep capture group: the time ;
                                           (regexpe)= [time.]


  's/.*?                 (?# lazy match of any character     )
    (                    (?# 1st capture group               )
      \d\d?              (?# 1 or 2 digits [day]             )
      [a-zA-Z]{3}        (?# 3 letters      [month]          )
    )                    (?# close 1st capture group         )
    [a-zA-Z]*            (?# more letters allowed            )
    (\d{2,4})            (?# 2nd capture group [year]        )
  /\1\2/x'               %*   keep date. type text    ;
                                           (regexpe)= [date.]

  '/^\s*[+-]?\d+\.\d+\s*$/'            (regexp) = [round()]

  '/^\s*[+-]?\d+\.?\s*$/'             (regexp) = _same_

  other                                  = .;

run;

data _null_;
  input X anynum.;
  if      X <  1e3 then putlog _INFILE_ $24. 'Num ' X= 16.4    ;
  else if X < 20e3 then putlog _INFILE_ $24. 'Date ' X= date9. ;
  else                  putlog _INFILE_ $24. 'Time ' X= time12.2;
cards;
01jun12
3.
-4.9
june
113:34:33.22
9:3:3.8
03noviembre2012
Meeting at 14:30 sharp
run;
```

Performance of Regular Expressions

While it is futile, due to the difference in scope, to try finding general rules when comparing the speed of regular expressions to that of other string functions, I cannot avoid providing an example since this is this book's object.

The simple example below seeks a repeated vowel in a string. In this case, the regular expression is 10% slower than the string functions. If the string is lengthened or if the match is closer to the end of the string, the regular expression will become faster than the string functions, and vice-versa. There is no general rule. Note how much code is needed to do this very simple task when using string functions.

```
data TEST;
STR='In our village, folks say God crumbles up the old moon into stars';
do I=1 to 1e6; output; end;
run;

data _null_;                   %* Reading RegEx can be unwieldly           ;
  set TEST;                    %* Thorough comments are most recommended ;
  where prxmatch('/([aeiou]) (?# find & capture a vowel   )
                 \1           (?# find capture group again )
                 /x'
               , STR);
run;

data _null_;
  set TEST;
  do while(1);
    POS=findc(STR,'aeiou',sum(POS,1)) ;       %* find a vowel              ;
    if POS=0 or POS=length(STR) then leave;   %* no more vowels to use   ;
    if char(STR,POS)=char(STR,POS+1) then do; %* next letter is the same;
    output; return; end;                      %* keep observation        ;
  end;
run;
```

Conclusion

When needing to manipulate character strings or to extract information from text files such as programs, log files, or documents, using regular expressions is a must. The power of regular expressions lies not in their speed but in the richness of their syntax. In order to write efficient programs that parse text, regular expressions are unsurpassed. This chapter provides you with the list of expressions supported by the SAS language.

Chapter 9

Conclusion

This is only the start

If you managed to reach this part of the book, congratulations. I know it must have been boring reading at times! However you should hopefully have learned a few things about how SAS works, what resources are used, and how to make the best use of them through the numerous ways SAS can be utilised and tweaked for improved performance.

More importantly, I hope that this book will have changed the way you write SAS code, the way you think even, why not, and that you will not only be considering how to solve problems, but also about to solve them efficiently.

This book cannot possibly cover all types of data, all types of processes and all types of hardware. You will have to test and get to know the environment you work in. So while I hope you have increased your technical knowledge, I mostly hope that you have fed a curiosity and an appetite for performance, and that this hunger will motivate you to make SAS processes more efficient.

The good thing with SAS is that everything is possible and there is something to learn every day. The better thing is that a skilled SAS user can make SAS processes very fast.

Much more can be said about the different ways performance can be boosted in SAS programs. If this book generates enough interest, I want to expand the topics presented and cover other areas of SAS programming.

In the meantime,

Keep learning, and good SAS coding!

Some interesting references

Hardware

Basic discussion on the evolution of CPU performance
http://www.tomshardware.com/forum/336310-28-processor-speeds-increasing

How to Maintain Happy SAS®9 Users
Margaret Crevar, SAS Institute Inc., Cary, NC
http://www.nesug.org/proceedings/nesug07/as/as04.pdf

Configuration and Tuning Guidelines for SAS®9 in Microsoft Windows Server 2008
Margaret Crevar, SAS Institute Inc., Cary, NC
http://support.sas.com/resources/papers/WindowsServer2008ConfigurationandTuning.pdf

Solving SAS® Performance Problems: Employing Host-Based Tools
Tony Brown, SAS Institute Inc., Dallas, TX
http://support.sas.com/rnd/scalability/papers/practicalperf.pdf

Peeking into Windows to Improve Performance
MP Welch, Solutions Architect, SAS Institute
http://www.scsug.org/SCSUGProceedings/2011/mpwelch1/Peeking%20into%20Windows%20to%20Improve%20Performance.pdf

SAS: Managing Memory and Optimizing System Performance
Jacek Czajkowski
https://dsgweb.wustl.edu/SSS/Managing%20Memory%20in%20SAS.ppt

Bit-rot
Bitrot and atomic COWs: Inside "next-gen" filesystems
http://arstechnica.com/information-technology/2014/01/bitrot-and-atomic-cows-inside-next-gen-filesystems/

Sorting

Advanced Performance Tuning Methods
http://support.sas.com/documentation/cdl/en/hostwin/63285/HTML/default/viewer.htm#advperf.htm

Selecting Efficient Sorting Strategies
http://web.utk.edu/sas/OnlineTutor/1.2/en/60477/m84/m84_1.htm

Getting the Best Performance from V9 Threaded PROC SORT
Scott Mebust - System Developer - Base Information Technology
http://support.sas.com/rnd/papers/sugi30/V9SORT.ppt

The SORT Procedure: Beyond the Basics
David Fickbohm, Homegain. Com, Emeryville, CA
www.lexjansen.com/wuss/2007/ApplicationsDevelopment/APP_Fickbaum_SortPrcedure.pdf

Performance Tools
*http://support.sas.com/documentation/cdl/en/hostwin/63285/HTML/default/viewer.htm#ntperfmon
.htm*

An Inside Look at Version 9 and Release 9.1 Threaded Base SAS® procedures
Robert Ray, SAS Institute Inc. Cary NC
http://www2.sas.com/proceedings/sugi28/282-28.pdf

Common Sense

Top 10 SAS coding efficiencies
Charu Shankar, 8 July 2013
http://blogs.sas.com/content/sastraining/2013/07/08/top-10-sas-coding-efficiencies/?appid=32489

Common Sense Tips and Clever Tricks for Programming with Extremely large data sets
Kathy Hardis Fraeman, United BioSource Corporation, Bethesda, MD
http://www.nesug.org/Proceedings/nesug08/ap/ap03.pdf

Large Scale Data Warehousing with the SAS(r) System
Tony Brown, Leigh Ihnen, JimCraig, SAS Institute Inc.
http://www2.sas.com/proceedings/sugi24/Dataware/p114-24.pdf

Advanced

Programmatically Measure SAS® Application Performance On Any Computer Platform With the New LOGPARSE SAS Macro
Michael A. Raithel, Westat, Rockville MD
http://sascommunity.org/wiki/Measure_SAS_Application_Performance_with_LogParse_Macro

Improving Your SAS Investment from the Ground Up: SAS 9.2 Enhancements That Help You Leverage Your Operating Environment
Clarke Thacher, SAS Institute Inc., Cary, NC
http://support.sas.com/rnd/papers/sgf2008/opsys92.pdf

A Hitchhiker's guide for performance assessment & benchmarking SAS® applications
Viraj Kumbhakarna, Anurag Katare, Cognizant Technology Solutions, Lake Hiawatha, NJ
http://support.sas.com/resources/papers/proceedings12/367-2012.pdf

Best Practices for Configuring your IO Subsystem for SAS®9 Applications
Margaret A. Crevar, Tony Brown, SAS Institute Inc.

http://support.sas.com/community/events/sastalks/presentations/BestPracticesIO.pdf

Performance Tuning & Sizing Guide for SAS Users and Sun System Administrators
William Kearns, Sun Microsystems Inc. & Tom Keefer, SAS Institute
http://unix.business.utah.edu/doc/applications/sas/Administration/SAS_on_Sun_Performance_Tuning_and_Sizing.pdf

Windows Features That Optimize Performance
http://support.sas.com/documentation/cdl/en/hostwin/63047/HTML/default/viewer.htm#p041tbb02reefnn1jmup3zo7tirr.htm

Scalable SAS Procedures
https://support.sas.com/rnd/scalability/procs/

Effectiveness and Cost of SAS® Compression
Hitesh Sharma, GCE Solutions, San Francisco, CA
http://support.sas.com/resources/papers/proceedings09/065-2009.pdf

SGIO

Improving SAS IO Throughput by Avoiding the Operating System File Cache
Leigh Ihnen and Mike Jones, SAS Institute Inc., Cary, NC
http://support.sas.com/resources/papers/proceedings09/327-2009.pdf

Frequently Asked Questions Regarding Storage Configurations
Margaret Crevar and Tony Brown, SAS Institute Inc.
http://support.sas.com/resources/papers/proceedings10/FAQforStorageConfiguration.pdf

Performance considerations
SAS 9.1 Companion for the Windows, Chapter 7
http://support.sas.com/documentation/onlinedoc/91pdf/sasdoc_91/base_hostwin_6974.pdf

Using SAS Files
SAS 9.2 Companion for UNIX Environments, Chapter 2
http://support.sas.com/documentation/cdl/en/hostunx/61879/PDF/default/hostunx.pdf

Achieving Better I/O Throughput Using SGIO in the Microsoft Windows Environment
http://support.sas.com/resources/papers/IOthruSGIO.pdf

Windows NT Server Configuration and Tuning for Optimal Server Performance
Susan E. Davis, Carl E. Ralston, Compaq Computer Corp., Cary, NC
http://www2.sas.com/proceedings/sugi26/p277-26.pdf

Solving Performance Problems in the SAS® Environment with SSD
Amadeus Software
http://www.amadeus.co.uk/sas-training/papers/12/1/36/solving-performance-problems-in-the-sas-environment-with-solid-state-drives.pdf

How to Increase I/O Throughput with SAS for Windows' SGIO Feature
Tracy Carver
http://support.sas.com/techsup/technote/ts710.pdf

SAS/CONNECT buffers

Prerequisites for Using TCP/IP under Windows
*http://support.sas.com/documentation/cdl/en/camref/65309/HTML/default/viewer.htm#n134g7al1t
2tabn13z3bb15nu7af.htm*

SPDE

Comparing the Default Base SAS Engine and the SPD Engine
*http://support.sas.com/documentation/cdl/en/engspde/62981/HTML/default/viewer.htm#n1cfsh8m
hovf18n1j3cv6s4yl4vy.htm*

Member lock is not available for [..] SPD Engine data set
http://support.sas.com/kb/18/467.html

Table joins

SASTRACE: Your Key to RDBMS Empowerment
Andrew Howell, ANJ Solutions Pty Ltd
https://support.sas.com/resources/papers/proceedings15/3269-2015.pdf

SAS(R) 9.3 SQL Procedure User's Guide: Improving Query Performance
*http://support.sas.com/documentation/cdl/en/sqlproc/63043/HTML/default/viewer.htm#n1wue1kaf
t1rlsn1v0y5m569besp.htm*

**New SAS® Performance Optimizations to Enhance Your SAS® Client and Solution Access
to the Database**
Mike Whitcher, SAS Institute, Cary, NC
https://support.sas.com/resources/papers/sgf2008/optimization.pdf

Add a Little Magic to Your Joins
Kirk Paul Lafler, Software Intelligence Corporation, Spring Valley, California
https://www.mwsug.org/proceedings/2012/S1/MWSUG-2012-S109.pdf

TS-553 "SQL Joins – The Long and The Short of It"
Paul Kent, SAS Institute Inc.
https://support.sas.com/techsup/technote/ts553.html

Regular Expressions

Comparing the Default Base SAS Engine and the SPD Engine
*http://support.sas.com/documentation/cdl/en/engspde/62981/HTML/default/viewer.htm#n1cfsh8m
hovf18n1j3cv6s4yl4vy.htm*

Customize - Regex Library Editor - Using Regular Expressions
*http://support.sas.com/documentation/onlinedoc/dfdmstudio/2.5/dmpdmsug/Content/dfU_
Cstm_RegEx_16003.html*

An Introduction to Perl Regular Expressions in SAS 9
Ron Cody, Robert Wood Johnson Medical School, Piscataway, NJ
http://www2.sas.com/proceedings/sugi29/265-29.pdf

Some Simple Perl Regular Expressions Examples in SAS® 9
Selvaratnam Sridharma, Census Bureau, Washington, D.C.
http://support.sas.com/resources/papers/proceedings10/089-2010.pdf

Taming Your Character Data with Regular Expressions in SAS® – Part I
Mary McCracken & James J. Van Campen, SRI International, Menlo Park, CA
*http://www.lexjansen.com/wuss/2004/data_warehousing/c_dwdb_taming_your_charac_p
1.pdf*

The Basics of the PRX Functions
David L. Cassell, Design Pathways, Corvallis, OR
http://www.wuss.org/proceedings09/09WUSSProceedings/papers/tut/TUT-Cassell.pdf

Perl Regular Expressions in SAS
Kevin McGowan , Constella Group, Durham, NC
http://analytics.ncsu.edu/sesug/2006/AP09_06.PDF